F

MW00873781

MISTAKEN IDENTITY

"I've read several books about addiction, but this one is much, much more than that! Although Paul tells his story of recovery beautifully, the book's greatest gift is how it leads us to discover the light of our own true being. Noiles believes that addiction is caused by deep emotional pain that creates an unlovable mistaken identity. Through recovery, gifted mentors, meditation, and a variety of spiritual practices, we grow into our "true identity" a beacon of love in this world. Paul's use of experts, research, personal stories, and transformative practices make for a fascinating read about addiction, rebirth, and joyful living. I highly recommend it!"
—**Gigi Langer, Ph.D. Psychological Studies in Education, Stanford University, author of *50 Ways to Worry Less Now: Reject Negative Thinking to Find Peace, Clarity, and Connection***

"Paul Noiles is the real deal, and *Mistaken Identity* tells the real story. We live in a world that is coming apart from substance use disorders—deaths of despair climb with no end in sight. The war on drugs has morphed into a war on people. The acute care, rinse-and-repeat treatment model systematically ignores 90% of the problem. It can get downright depressing for those of us on the front lines. Thank God for people like Paul and books like *Mistaken Identity*. His comprehensive exploration of substance use disorders and the clear articulation of holistic recovery is top tier. Our programs serve thousands of people each year, and I am frequently asked: "What book should I read to learn more about addiction and recovery?" Finally, I have a recommendation that I can make without reservation. *Mistaken Identity* will get the job done and then some. Thank you, Paul, for this fantastic work."
—**Richard Jones: MA, MBA, LCAS, CCS, CEAP, SAP, CAI, certified EMDR Trauma Therapist**

"One of the great challenges people face in trying to overcome addiction is that their approach to finding freedom originates from within the same manner of thinking that led to the addiction in the first place. So, inevitably a person's efforts to free her or himself do not work. With *Mistaken Identity*, Paul Noiles shares key insights and inspiration that originate not from within the addictive mindset, but from beyond it. Paul has had an awakening from the darkness of addiction, and it is detailed here as he touches on the many modalities of healing and ancient teachings which became a part of the tapestry of his recovery. From detailing the 10 layers of mistaken identity to providing seven practices of awakening, Paul has given us something practical, applicable and relevant. *Mistaken Identity* can guide a reader toward the Truth. I recommend it to anyone looking to move beyond addiction and thrive."

—Tommy Rosen: Addiction Expert, Founder of Recovery 2.0, Yoga Teacher, author of *Recovery 2.0: Move Beyond Addiction and Upgrade Your Life*

MISTAKEN IDENTITY

A Sacred Journey from Addiction to Awakening

PAUL NOILES

Tellwell Talent
tellwell.ca

ISBN
978-0-2288-1497-9 (Paperback)
978-0-2288-1498-6 (eBook)

Permissions have been granted from the following to use their material:

Ferentzy, Peter. *Dealing with Addiction: Why the 20th Century Was Wrong.* Self-published, May 9, 2011.

Maté, Gabor. *In the Realm of Hungry Ghosts: Close Encounters with Addiction.* Random House Canada, 2009.

Rosen, Tommy. *Recovery 2.0: Move Beyond Addiction and Upgrade Your Life.* Hay House, Inc., October 21, 2014.

Szalavitz, Maia. *Unbroken Brain: A Revolutionary New Way of Understanding Addiction.* Picador St. Martin's Press, April 5, 2016.

Richard L. (Rich) Jones contributed three pages about the myth of hitting rock bottom and family recovery.

I want to thank all these brilliant minds for their inspiring words that touch the souls of many. Words are important!

First printing 2021

To order, or to learn more, please visit **paulnoiles.com** and facebook.com/noiles.paul and instagram.com/paulnoiles/

Recommendations

"Thank you from the bottom of my heart for your part in my recovery! I celebrated seven years sober in April, and I could not have done it without you."

Karen Hope, Vancouver Island

"Paul is an incredible and intuitive coach who meets you where you are with options and workable tools to help work through chaos and health issues and push forward."

Carrie Lea Lang, Pennsylvania

"I had worked with therapists for so long, trying to stop self-harming and addictive habits, without getting to the bottom of it all. Until I worked with Paul."

Jennifer Kip, California

"Paul's approach focuses on self-acceptance and includes honest discussion, straight-talking feedback, and guidance on what to do to move forward. ... I recommend Paul as a down-to-earth, compassionate and knowledgeable mentor for anyone who needs help letting go of a lifetime of patterns and beliefs that aren't serving them."

Millie Garnet, Washington

"I learned about my true essence from Paul and applied it to my mental, physical, and spiritual self where it has manifested itself in many ways."

Logan Legiehn, Winnipeg

"Selfless, warm, and wise, Paul held the space for my grief and supported me. His presence made it possible for me to fully dive into the pain I felt. Only then could I reconnect to my truth. I wish everyone suffering from emotional pain had someone like Paul."

Nadja Franke, Germany

"Paul's ability to keep it simple and get right to the core so easily was truly amazing and helped me more than I could imagine."

Debe Bair, Oregon

"Paul did not tell me what to do ... but gave me the ability to let go of a lot of fear and make my own decisions ... Without him, I may not have dared going in [the] direction which has been so good for me. ... I recommend Paul to others."

Inger Alice Rekk, Norway

"Paul blew my mind and [connected] some of the missing pieces of the "meditation puzzle" that had been absent in my journey of self-discovery. With Paul's help, the pieces fell into place ... Thank you from the bottom of my heart."

Lisa Seeley, Australia

"Years of therapy did not compare to the simple tools Paul gave me. I discovered that I was no longer addicted to substances, but addicted to suffering. Paul's teachings helped me realize that at my core, I'm not the pain or Mistaken Identity. Love is who I am."

Lisa Parsons, Toronto

You can find more recommendations at paulnoiles.com

CONTENTS

ACKNOWLEDGMENTS

Mistaken Identity would not have been possible without the many individuals who held their light for me along the path: my mentor the Reverend Lorraine Trout, mom and dad, sister Lana, brother Dave, best friend Shane Hannam, and my close friends and brothers in recovery Jason Rock, Justin Hodgson, Daniel Petros, Ivan Krasavsev, Michael Lalonde and Dwayne Cameron.

Thanks to my former sponsor Chris D. and Kevin Hastings who gave me the extra support I needed to finish the book.

I will be forever grateful to Frank Barlow for not only believing in me but for investing his money in a first-time author. I could not have done it without you.

Much appreciation to Tommy Rosen for his essential insight of my first draft and to Rich Jones for his contributions.

I offer my gratitude to Liz McDougall, writer and friend, whose support kept me on task, and to Glenda Rankin for helping with the graphics for the front and back covers.

Thanks to Jennifer Chapin from Tellwell Publishing for her patience and to my freelance editor extraordinaire, Anita LeBlanc, who put in countless hours.

I also extend my gratitude and thanks for the generous early edits and support from Steven Curson, Gigi Langer, Linda Mills, Corinna Dixon, Patricia Harding, Andy Sicking, Becky Durango, Lisa Seeley, Cheryl Cormier, Jean Van Kleek, Mercedes Grant Hopkins, Elizabeth Kipp, Cindy Di Nunzio McArthur, Mira Rao, Liv Victor and Jenn Crawford.

My adorable Chihuahua, Sharona, whose love sustained me as I wrote and rewrote, deserves a note of appreciation as well.

Finally, I dedicate this book to the Reverend Darrell Gudmundson, another mentor, a father figure, and an exceptional author, with one of the most brilliant minds I've ever known. Before his passing in 2013, he encouraged me to write and never stop. He gave me the confidence to write this book.

FROM THE REVEREND LORRAINE TROUT

I have had the honor of working with Paul as his mentor for the last twenty-six years. This book is about a courageous journey of a soul in the depth and fullness of human experience. Paul came into this life with the awareness of deeper meaning but became distracted by worldly things.

Throughout his book, Paul shares the depth and rawness of his journey with a courage and honesty rarely seen in the world today. Paul's sharing of his experiences continues to restore hope for many in the grip of addiction or any other type of suffering.

Here, you'll discover your relationship with your thoughts and uncover the disempowering beliefs from trauma, pain, and shame that have held you hostage in what Paul calls mistaken identity. Through Paul's eyes, you'll become aware of the most profound inner reality, helping you see beyond your current suffering to a more authentic and satisfying reality.

Writing this book changed Paul's life, and I am sure reading it could change yours. Today, Paul serves humanity by serving others who suffer as he did.

Reverend Lorraine Trout

WELCOME

There was a single reason for my addiction—I didn't like who I thought I was. Substances and other behaviors only temporarily quieted and soothed the painful messages ruling me since I was a boy, ones with roots in my mistaken identity.

Whether you're in long-term recovery, new to recovery, or a friend or relative of someone suffering from addiction or other negative behaviors, this book can help you find a deeper level of freedom.

The principles here apply to every kind of addiction—from drugs, alcohol, food, and cigarettes, to behaviors such as sex, codependency, shopping, and gambling. They also work for "thought addictions" (perfectionism, compulsive thinking, and worrying), "emotion addictions" (anger, rage, guilt, suffering, and fear), "activity addictions" (crime, exercise, and overwork), and the currently socially accepted Internet addiction (social media, video games, emails, and texting).

My ultimate hope is that you exchange the painful work of sustaining your current suffering for the challenging but life-affirming and non-negotiable work of awakening. You will lose the desire to self-medicate while finding your true essence of love, peace, and joy, just as I did.

One Love,
Paul Noiles

PREFACE

A STORY OF AFFIRMATION

꧁ ꧂

It's not to "never surrender" but to "always surrender."

꧁ ꧂

I had been diligently writing this book's early draft for six months and getting ready to go to work at a treatment center outside Toronto when everything changed. *Everything!*

January 20, 2015

Believing I'd return home the next day, I arrived on a cold morning at St. Paul's Hospital to undergo a non-invasive corrective surgery. However, as the surgeon cut deep into my neck to better access the area, he punctured my esophagus. To prevent movement and aid healing, the surgical team stapled my chin to my chest.

For the next seven days, I was under massive sedation in the intensive care unit. I could barely focus my eyes, move my body, or speak properly. My brain felt paralyzed. I could sense when someone was in the room and hear their every word, but I could not respond coherently—and sometimes I could not respond at all. Doctors, nurses, Reverend Lorraine, and other friends tried to pull me out of the dark abyss, but I remained trapped in the tunnel with my thoughts, visions, and imagination.

While in this state of consciousness, I fought to stay awake, reasoning that I would die if I fell asleep. I began to visually order my thoughts into short video clips and pictures to keep myself awake. This experience of directing my thoughts granted me a more in-depth understanding that not only was I *not* my thoughts but that I had the power to change my thoughts at will. What a revelation!

Yet, I struggled to replace the increasingly dark and more disturbing images with pleasant ones and to maintain consciousness.

Completely exhausted on day seven, I could no longer stay awake. I knew from my spiritual work that death was only the letting go of the physical body. I stopped fighting and surrendered my life to Spirit.

Suddenly, there was a flash of bright light in my mind and a beautiful voice asking me what I wanted to do before I left. The voice gave me a strong sense of absolute comfort and safety.

I answered that I wanted to pray for other people who were suffering and struggling. The divine voice told me to do so.

As I began to pray, majestic jagged mountains, each with a single candle burning brilliantly at its top, suddenly surrounded me. As I continued to pray, the towering mountains rose slowly and then with increasing speed, as the light from the candles grew in brightness and intensity. I had never before experienced such profound joy, such a sense of oneness, and such indescribable feelings of love.

As the mountains faded, the bright, beautiful light consumed me. I thanked the Great Love for my glorious life and *let go.*

After I slept peacefully for ten hours, Reverend Lorraine, who had been at my bedside for days repeating mantras and affirmative prayers, asked me where I'd been. Surprised to be alive, I asked her to capture my story on paper and then told it to her.

Discharged from the hospital three days later, I reread my book's original pages and knew the content was not from my heart. I enthusiastically destroyed those eighty pages. Seizing my laptop, I wrote, "All is well with my soul."

As I reflected on those days in the ICU, I recalled my stubbornness and persistence to hang onto life when the only solution was to *surrender*. The decision to let go was the first time I had experienced the complete death of my ego-self, a death that made it possible to view my life and recovery from a deeper state of awakened consciousness.

For the next two months, I wept with joy from the realization that I had always been one with Love [God], not only during the surgery but during the many years of addiction and relapse. As I pondered why I had been blocked from Love during all those years of addiction, it became clear that I had mistaken my identity.

Had my surgery not taken a turn for the worse, I would not have received the mistaken identity concept from the heart of consciousness and found a new, more authentic direction for my life and my book.

It took a lifetime of self-discovery and four years to write this book. If someone were to ask me what was the most meaningful awakening for me, I would say, "Compassion, more compassion, and deeper compassion for myself and others."

I hope these pages bring this compassion to you.

All Addictions Come Out of Pain.
All Recovery Comes Out of Love.

–Paul Noiles

SECTION A

A NEW LOOK AT ADDICTION AND RECOVERY

NEW DEFINITIONS OF ADDICTION

ᘉ◎ ◎ᘏ

*"When I grow up, I want to be an addict
or alcoholic," said no one ever.*

ᘉ◎ ◎ᘏ

The American Society of Addiction Medicine (ASAM) released a new, more comprehensive definition of addiction in 2011, one that made headlines worldwide, highlighting dependence as a chronic brain disorder, not a behavioral problem involving too much alcohol, drugs, gambling, or sex. It was the first time the American Society of Addiction Medicine had taken an official position that addiction isn't solely related to problematic substance use, citing addiction as a primary chronic disease, not the result of psychiatric problems. Dr. Raju Hajela, past president of the Canadian Society of Addiction Medicine, added,

> There is longstanding controversy over whether people with addiction have choice over anti-social and dangerous behaviors. The disease creates distortions in thinking, feelings, and perceptions, which drive people to behave in ways that are not understandable to others around them.
>
> Simply put, addiction is not a choice. Addictive behaviors are a manifestation of the disease, not a cause.

According to trauma and addiction expert Dr. Gabor Maté, addiction has the key features of a disease in that it has symptoms

3

and causes physical/mental debility and relapse. However, Dr. Maté doesn't believe the disease model alone explains addiction. In his book, *In The Realm of the Hungry Ghost*, he warns,

> We need to avoid the trap of believing addiction can be reduced to the actions of brain chemicals or nerve circuits or any other kind of neurobiological, psychological, or sociological data ... Addiction is a complex condition, a complex interaction between human beings and their environment.
>
> We need to view it simultaneously from many different angles—or, at least, while examining it from one angle, we need to keep the others in mind. Addiction has biological, chemical, neurological, psychological, medical, emotional, social, political, economic, and spiritual underpinnings—and perhaps others ... To get anywhere near a complete picture, we must keep shaking the kaleidoscope to see what other patterns emerge.[1]

Dr. Maté believes that addiction's primary source is trauma and emotional loss in early childhood, not genes. He further believes that every person with an addiction has trauma, but not every person with trauma will develop an addiction.

Maia Szalavitz, the author of the *New York Times* best-selling book *Unbroken Brain: A Revolutionary New Way of Understanding Addiction*, offers another perspective:

> Addiction is better characterized as a learning or developmental disorder than as a brain disease. While those who support the brain disease concept see it as a way of reducing stigma, in actual fact, this idea can increase fear and hatred of addicts

because the notion of "brain damage" suggests permanence and poor odds for recovery. What addiction actually does in the brain is similar to what love does—it strongly wires in new memories and pushes us to seek certain experiences. This is not "damage" or "destruction". When we understand addiction as one more type of neurodiversity—not always a disability, sometimes even a source of strength—we'll really cut stigma.[2]

Professor and psychologist Dr. Bruce K. Alexander in *The Globalization of Addiction: A Study in the Poverty of the Spirit* delivers a convincing case that addiction is manufactured by economic globalization and the social dislocation that inevitably comes with capitalism. He says we shouldn't ask about what kind of individual weakness, vulnerability, or drug exposure leads some to addiction, but instead why our current society makes it so difficult and painful for so many to avoid addiction.

Dr. Alexander calls this phenomenon "the dislocation theory of addiction," which looks beyond the individual and identifies addiction as an "adaptive response" to broader societal problems, ones that dislocate the individual from a sense of identity, belonging, meaning, purpose, and value.[3]

Like Dr. Maté, Ms. Szalavitz, Dr. Alexander, and the American Society of Addiction Medicine, I believe that the causes of addiction include trauma, economic globalization, brain conditions, and a learning or developmental disorder and that recovery is always possible.

This book is not about another definition of addiction. It's about a solution.

∞

Is Addiction a Family Disease?

The family members, partners, and friends of those with an addiction often mistakenly believe they have no part in the disease or its healing. They are frequently unaware that their behavior may be hindering the recovery process. This fallacy presents the biggest challenge for those in a relationship with someone in addiction—their denial.

I often saw this while facilitating the family group at a treatment center. When I explained that denial and addiction are family issues where everyone has a part in the healing, many looked bewildered. Some even glared at me.

The more family members with unresolved issues try to help, the more the person with the addiction resists; the result is more pain for everyone. For instance, if a mother or father has not dealt with their substance abuse or their issues from growing up with an alcoholic parent, the parent will be of little help.

We can't give what we don't have. Family members must realize that enabling includes dispensing money, chastising, consoling, or guilting or shaming. Enabling can be dangerous and may prolong addiction.

The best advice to family members or friends of someone with an addiction is to love them right where they are, without judgment or a complete understanding, while enforcing clear boundaries, accountability, and consequences. If you genuinely want to help a loved one with an addiction, begin your own healing. Be the change you wish to see in the relationship. Your healing can produce a profound impact from the resulting energy of love.

Finally, I cannot stress enough the importance of parents doing the vital work of letting go of guilt and shame for the things they did or didn't do. Why? Because nobody wants to be somebody else's failure. As long as parents carry guilt or shame about their kids, they see their failures every time they look at them. Who wants to be somebody else's failure?

∞

A Declaration of Commitment to Truth, Love, and Peace

"I have a condition called addiction. It's no different than having cancer or diabetes or any other illness or disease. I am not a bad person. I am the timeless, eternal Love beyond it."

THE SEEKER

My quest was and still is to seek the truth. It saved my life.
I am confident it will save anyone who truly desires it.

The genesis of the Mistaken Identity model began when I read
Deepak Chopra's *Overcoming Addiction*:

> I see the addict as a seeker, albeit a misguided
> one. The addict is a person in quest of pleasure,
> perhaps even a kind of transcendent experience—
> and I want to emphasize that this kind of seeking
> is extremely positive. The addict is looking in the
> wrong places, but he is going after something
> very important, and we cannot afford to ignore
> the meaning of his search. At least initially, the
> addict hopes to experience something wonderful,
> something that transcends an unsatisfactory
> or even an intolerable everyday reality. There's
> nothing to be ashamed of in this impulse. On the
> contrary, it provided a foundation for true hope
> and real transformation.[4]

I could see how the motivations of the misguided seeker were
part of my history. Although I was working the twelve steps with a
sponsor, attending regular meetings, and being of service, I relapsed
repeatedly. Instinctively, I knew the misguided seeker's concept was
the key to my recovery, but I didn't understand how to access it.

Later, after a decade of pain and suffering, I found two quotes that expanded my understanding; Eckhart Tolle's, "Every addiction starts with pain and ends with pain," and Dr. Gabor Maté's, "Ask not why the addiction, but why the pain?" These highly respected men did not identify the person or substance but pain as the main component for addiction. It was an a-ha moment that led me to further inquiry.

What does someone with addiction believe about themselves when in pain? After contemplating the question, I realized I had always thought I was the pain—that any negative emotion I experienced was because of my flaws and lack of worth. This toxic shame continuously fueled my addiction, made relapse predictable, and recovery impossible. I was startled by this discovery. A short time later, while meditating, I sensed higher consciousness asking if I was the pain. I said I wasn't. Higher consciousness then asked who was experiencing the pain?

I realized then that I had created a false self to deal with my psychological, physical, and emotional pain. Therefore, there must be an authentic self beyond the pain. From these powerful questions came the mistaken identity catchphrase: *Addiction is about pain, the pain of not knowing or liking who we think we are.*

∞

For me and millions like me, using substances or behaviors was a way to temporarily quiet and soothe the mistaken identity's painful messages.

Who would have ever thought the solution to overcoming addiction and relapse could be found in answering one simple, profound question: "Who am I?"

Peeling away the layers of 'who we are not' allows us to investigate and discover the innate essence of 'who we are.' This process of spiritual awakening requires understanding, compassion, and vulnerability. It is painful to peel away the layers, but through it we dismantle our mistaken identity and wake up to our true selves.

By letting go of the person we thought we were, we become the person we truly are.

It's a painful process to wake up spiritually, but the results are well worth it.

While I believe the mistaken identity is the primary cause of addiction, genetic factors (addiction in the family tree) and co-occurring disorders (formerly known as dual diagnosis or dual disorders) may also play a part. An estimated 37 percent of alcohol abusers and 53 percent of drug abusers have at least one serious mental illness.[5]

∞

Attachment and Authenticity

Think about it. The minute we come out of the womb, we need attachment (human connection: closeness, nurturing, cared for, protected from harm). It's a non-negotiable human need wired into our nervous system for survival. Humans need safe, secure attachments for mental, emotional, physical, and spiritual well-being.

If a child does not have secure and safe attachments, they will throw their authentic self out the window. It's why the need for attachment will always trump authenticity in childhood.

Children in stressful environments will have to develop coping mechanisms to survive. They often create false narratives about themselves, their family, and their surroundings to deal with their pain. Over time, the stress and false stories change who they are, and, like a snowball growing in size and momentum as it rolls down a hill, the narrative and belief continue into adulthood.

I had to disconnect from my essence, and my mistaken identity was the way to survive, not something to be ashamed of. However, it created a painful dilemma: I desperately wanted connection, but I feared the possibility of being rejected. I was in a fight with myself, and fear always seemed to win.

Looking back at those painful years, all I ever wanted was some sense of family, and my substance of choice took away that pain. Addiction provided a fake sense of connection and family, which sounds absurd. Of course, I was completely unaware that all of this was going on.

∞

All addictions and negative behaviors alter our perceptions of reality and affect our ability to be honest with ourselves. We seek relationships that serve our selfish interests or promote our agenda to use our substance of choice. I felt like two different people, believing I was simultaneously less than others and better than others. As people sometimes say in twelve-step meetings, "we are egomaniacs with an inferiority complex."

∞

Reframing Addiction

Those with addiction are in a place that most people without addiction can never understand. We can either continue to suffer, live in misery, and hate who we

> There is nothing to fix in anyone, only to awaken to their true selves.

are, or we can get into recovery, do the work, discover the great Love that resides within us, and have an incredible life.

If you had to go to the extremes of suffering, you will likely experience an equal, opposite *light* when you wake up and recover. Just as in Newton's third law of physics, "For every action, there is an equal

> Learn more about Reframing Addiction.
> https://youtu.be/p1BTMOq5AXk

11

and opposite reaction." This experience is what happened to many of my friends and me. It's the reason we can give away what we have so effortlessly.

A Declaration of Commitment to Truth, Love, and Peace

"I choose to do the vital work of peeling the layers of my mistaken identity. My false self will fade away, allowing me to step into my true nature, the energy of Love."

MY ADDICTION BEGINS

*Everyone can understand addiction because everyone has
searched outside themselves to deal with their pain.*

1988

All addictions provide some positive functions, or we would
not have done them in the first place. For me, I was twenty-six
years old when the seeds of
addiction, planted when I
was a child, began to sprout
at a staff Christmas party.
As I was drinking a cold
beer, I took a hit off a joint
and suddenly felt euphoric
in ways marijuana had
never made me feel. I saw
a woman across the room,
rolling another joint and
spiking it with cocaine.

> "Our brains register any kind of
> pleasure in the same way, whether
> they originate with a psychoactive
> drug, a monetary reward, a sexual
> encounter, or a satisfying meal. In
> the brain, pleasure has a distinct
> signature: the release of the
> neurotransmitter dopamine in the
> nucleus accumbens, a cluster of
> nerve cells lying underneath the
> cerebral cortex. Dopamine release
> in the nucleus accumbens is so
> consistently tied with pleasure
> that neuroscientists refer to the
> region as the brain's pleasure
> center."
> *~ Harvard Health Publishing*[6]

Enjoying my new
cocaine-powered marijuana
high, I decided to snort
my first line. I felt whole,
connected, unafraid of
others, and at peace for the first time in my life. I remember
saying to my best friend, Rickie, that I now understood the allure
of cocaine.

Little did I know that recovery would require discovering why I was disconnected and not at peace with myself; it had nothing to do with the substance of my desire.

Getting high became the only way to stop the never-ending stream of self-defeating talk in my head. At times, I thought if I couldn't use drugs to numb the feelings, I would rather die. It sounds ridiculous, but individuals in the grip of addiction find their brains hijacked, so even the most outrageous belief and behavior seem viable.

∞

What does your addiction do for you? How does it serve you? These are essential questions we must ask ourselves. Our answers will help us discover how to get our needs met without using our substance of choice.

∞

My Addiction Progresses

My consumption of cocaine slowly increased from binge use on weekends to rarely being able to turn it down.

Externally, I had an affluent, successful life. I was a partner in a lucrative advertising business. I had a wife, family, and friends who loved me. However, internally I felt empty, worthless. My success only brought more misery because I felt like an imposter. My wife, Sandra, was becoming more and more disappointed with my drug use, as I often arrived home from another crazy night just as she was waking up for work. She had no idea how bad it was.

After reluctantly ending my business partnership, I accepted a marketing director position at a high-tech company that sold telecommunication equipment to police and fire departments across North America.

At a trade show in Memphis, I returned to the hotel for a nap before dinner with the company president and team. As I showered and dressed for the evening, I decided to score some blow before meeting them. I hopped into a taxi and asked the cabbie to drive me to the hood, where I met two dealers standing on the corner. When I opened the package I bought from them, I saw it wasn't the cocaine I'd expected, but crack cocaine, a drug I thought was only for losers. When I asked for my money back, the dealer laughed and lifted his shirt to show his gun. After apologizing (the gun had humbled me), he pointed out the corner store where I would find the gear I needed to smoke.

The cab driver took me to the restaurant where I was to meet my team. I walked behind a nearby building, pulled out the paraphernalia, and began to put the pipe together. As I was about to light up, I saw two cops on mountain bikes. I threw everything in my pocket and began to walk toward the restaurant.

I began to cross at the four-way stop in front of the restaurant when I saw the bike cops advancing with two police cruisers behind them. There were flashing lights, blaring sirens, and cops with guns pointed at me, one of whom quickly slammed me spread-eagle onto the hood of the cop car.

The possible consequences filled my mind: spending months trying to get back to Canada after an arrest in the U.S., losing my wife and job, and having a criminal record. I promised myself in the back of the cruiser that I would never use cocaine again.

One of the cops asked me why I was in Memphis. After I told him, he said sarcastically, "You're here to sell telecommunication equipment to police, and you're out buying crack cocaine. You're a dumb ass, motherfucker."

I didn't understand why they were taking me to my hotel instead of jail. The cop taking off my handcuffs cleared this up by saying, "I don't know if you're lucky or dumb. The cab driver called us right after taking you to the hood, where you could have been robbed or killed. You didn't buy cocaine. They sold you wax, so I can't arrest you. You are the luckiest and dumbest Canadian I ever met."

I arrived at the convention center the next morning after a sleepless night, praying no one had seen my arrest. After the president asked me why I hadn't shown up for dinner, I told him I had needed to do important final prep work for the show.

I returned to Canada a week later. The next weekend, I got high.

∞

1994

I met Joanne, an upscale, married woman with two small children. She sold drugs to support her addiction. She was a backup for when my dealer was unavailable. After she hooked me up with an eight ball, she invited me to a party. After snorting my third line, I looked up and saw her shooting up. When I asked her what the hell she was doing, she explained snorting was not possible anymore because she'd destroyed the lining of her nose. I left thinking that she was one sick, twisted addict, and I felt terrible for her children. My denial was epic!

Two months later, she pulled out a clean needle and offered it to me. I decided to try it "just once." I knew my life would never be the

> "Different methods of administration can influence how likely it is for a drug to lead to addiction. Smoking a drug or injecting it intravenously, as opposed to swallowing it as a pill, for example, generally produces a faster, stronger dopamine signal and is more likely to lead to drug misuse."
> -Harvard Health Publishing

same from that moment because shooting up took away all the pain inside me with an unprecedented high.

While getting high was a trip to heaven, coming down was a plunge to hell. I quickly became an intravenous cocaine junkie, overdosing regularly.

∞

My marriage ended in 1995, and my addiction spiraled, especially when I found out my soon-to-be ex-wife was dating a police officer she eventually would marry.

∞

In 1996, I discovered a "license to print money" after founding a new marketing company to promote fitness centers across Canada. My easy access to cash, combined with living alone, sent me reeling further into my addiction.

By 2002, I knew I had to quit the needle before an overdose killed me. My addicted mind saw smoking crack as harm reduction! Drugs no longer numbed the pain, but I continued to "chase the ghost" of my drug use's early days, all while using delusional stories to help me psychologically survive.

> My delusional "survival" story went something like this, "Society is a bunch of puppets controlled by materialism, power, and fear, and I am a maverick. Being a maverick, I do whatever I want—wake up when I want, use drugs whenever I want, make money (illegally) whenever I want, have crazy sex whenever I want. Look at me, fuckers! I do not live by the rubbish rules of the world. I am living like a rock star, just not with fame and fortune."

Blaming the world and the absence of any real responsibility in my life increased my excuses, and, in turn, opportunities to use. I'd "talk the talk" to friends about taking responsibility for my actions when my real plan was to win them over and justify my position. If left untreated, my "life-threatening progressive condition" would have killed me.

There can be no recovery or expansion of consciousness until we take full responsibility for ourselves. Without it, many go to the depths of hell or die. I know today that I am not taking responsibility when I feel restless or down.

∞

A Declaration and Commitment to Truth, Love, and Peace

"I no longer choose to believe in old limitations and lack. I now see myself as the Universe sees me—perfect, whole, and complete. I am worthy of the best in life. I will step into my light."

SECTION B

THE TEN LAYERS OF MISTAKEN IDENTITY

Think of your mistaken identity as an onion with many layers. As we peel away the layers, we uncover the essential truth of who we are: the eternal I Am (Pure Awareness), the embodiment of Love, Peace, and Joy. Remove your disguise, and claim your freedom with the following affirmation:

I am not a Victim—I Am.
I am not My Pain and Trauma—I Am.
I am not Toxic Shame—I Am.
I am not Rock Bottom—I Am.
I am not My Thoughts—I Am.
I am not My Emotions and Feelings—I Am.
I am not My Body—I Am.
I am not My Beliefs—I Am.
I am not My Personality—I Am.
I am not My Fears—I Am.

Further explore this knowing to experience the miracle of who you really are. It will be the end of your relapses and the beginning of your lasting and joyful recovery.

We can never fully know who we are, just as a knife can't cut itself, and fire can't burn itself. But we can get close enough to experience our true essence —Love, Peace, and Joy.

LAYER ONE

VICTIM

～⊚ ⊚～

We must decide we are worth saving.

⊚～ ⊚⌐

Being rescued was a fantasy I carried well into adulthood, a story where my father would ride in on a white horse and lovingly save me from the horrors of addiction. Instead, I perceived abandonment when I told Dad that I had a severe cocaine addiction, and he pulled away. I capitalized on my perception of rejection by increasing my drug use, self-righteously savoring my resentment and victim mentality.

Being angry at the world allowed me to hide the actual pain of feeling unworthy. My denial and refusal to accept reality fueled the addiction. Eventually, I understood it wasn't my father's or anyone else's responsibility to save me. It was mine.

When I realized *no one was coming to save me*, I cried, my whole body shaking. I finally admitted, deep in my heart, that I was terrified of being unlovable and alone. It was gut-wrenching. Spiritual awakenings work this way.

After my tears and processing the pain, I experienced a vast letting go and new freedom. I felt the real me for the first time as I looked back at the hurt little boy I'd been. I felt the presence of a loving power, and I knew deep within my

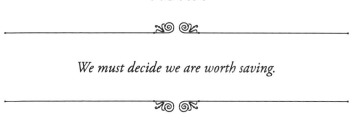

Learn more in No One Is Coming to Save Us.
https://youtu.be/k7gF4H7NRmg

21

heart, everything would be okay from that day forward. I was finally ready to live.

Motivation

In the past, I felt I needed motivation to change. I later discovered that waiting for inspiration was a self-defeating and dangerous strategy.

Evolution designed our fearful brains to protect us from difficult, uncomfortable, frightening, stressful situations, and change is exactly that. It's the real reason motivation never arrives for so many. Change frequently only happens for most people when the pain of staying the same is greater than the pain of change.

Waiting has killed many people with addictions because they die before they felt motivated to change. Some were my friends. Waiting is merely another false belief, another excuse to avoid responsibility.

Today, whenever I feel uncomfortable, I feel excited. Even though change is difficult and frustrating, and I feel as if I might

Learn more in Motivation: A Bullshit Story. https://youtu.be/PJr8JFENOco

fail, I also know that it's the only way to become the best version of myself. We must take a leap of faith and do it!

Get comfortable with being uncomfortable. It will prepare you to handle any situation.

Finding Meaning for Our Suffering

Once I let go of waiting to be saved, a new question emerged from the heart of consciousness: "How can I use my years of suffering to make the world a better place?"

I took the pain, regret, and loss and found meaning by sharing my experiences with others and through selfless service. Today, I see my horrific suffering, not as my enemy but as my teacher.

Choosing our reaction is how we honor our suffering and discover that Love is who we are. But it often takes many years to get over the hardwired fantasy of looking for a savior.

We alone must decide to step into the fullness of life. It's a difficult process that allows no excuses because each excuse makes it easier to make another excuse.

> Addiction is not a choice; however, recovery is 100 percent our responsibility.

The more I invested in my excuses, the more I blamed myself, others, and situations. When I stopped making excuses, I was finally able to feel empowered and begin the work of recovery.

∞

The "Great" Purpose

I once believed a successful life, and others' respect and admiration would be mine if I could find a great purpose. I'd heard this repeatedly from world consciousness, friends, family, and many so-called spiritual teachers. At times, I thought I'd found it after years of pursuit only to remain miserable, confused, and addicted as I continued to operate out of the ego of my mistaken identity.

I had no idea who I was, which made it easy to find many false purposes, waste time, and still feel unfulfilled, unhappy, purposeless, and prone to relapse.

Eventually, I let go of my pursuit of purpose and devoted my time to finding my authentic self. By focusing on my awakening (internal purpose) and the present moment, my outer purpose began to naturally show-up. Go figure!

When we connect to Source, stop basing our lives on others' opinions, look into the abyss, do the work, and fully engage in living life, our purpose, authentic self, and recovery arrive naturally.

∞

Discipline

Discipline used to be a dirty word for me and many of us who were physically hurt or shamed or threatened (fear) or criticized as little

> "There is always light, if we are brave enough to see it. If only we are brave enough to be it."
> ~Amanda Gorman

children into discipline. None of those ways will ever motivate a child or even an adult into lasting discipline because it will eventually unravel over the long haul.

The art of compassionate discipline is a learned behavior that must come from a place of practice, authenticity, compassion, patients, truth, and love. I would not be here today if not for the compassionate discipline I learned from those who inspired and motivated me, especially in my early recovery and awakening years.

To achieve lasting recovery or any ongoing change, we have to become a different person, and that requires great discipline to do whatever it takes to wake-up to our true self. There are no secret formulas, hacks, or quick fixes, and there is no one coming to save us. We must crush our rescue fantasy, decide we are worth saving, and take full responsibility for our recovery and awakening which requires compassionate discipline.

Bravely I faced my demons, mistaken identity, and took the required discipline to get to know the real me. Even though I was scared to death of what I might find under my disguise.

∞

A Declaration and Commitment to Truth, Love, and Peace

"I am not a victim. I am worthy of the best in life, but I must stop waiting for someone to save me. I will be brave, get comfortable with being uncomfortable, and do the work of recovery because I am worth it."

LAYER TWO

PAIN AND TRAUMA

꒐◎ ◎꒐

Pain is at the heart of all addictions.

꒐◎ ◎꒐

Most people choose to stick with the misery of pain and suffering instead of the unknown of change. We rationalize that at least we know how to "manage" pain with our addiction of choice, unwittingly enhancing the very feelings we are trying to crush. But, no matter how we slice and dice it, it's not management—it's denial.

Sogyal Rinpoche wrote in *The Tibetan Book of Living and Dying*, "Whatever you do, do not try to escape your pain. Be with it." The great Sufi mystic and poet Rumi wrote, "The cure for pain is in the pain."

Unfortunately, the only way to lessen or eliminate pain and suffering is first to stop using, then cradle and embrace the pain and suffering. Only then can we observe what it's all about and learn healthy ways to be okay. Trust me; I tried everything to avoid the pain.

No substance or activity is addictive in

> "Drugs, in short, do not make anyone into an addict, any more than food makes a person into a compulsive eater. There has to be a pre-existing vulnerability."
> ~Dr. Gabor Maté, physician, addiction and trauma expert, author

and of itself. Alcohol does not make someone an alcoholic. Cocaine does not make someone a cocaine addict. Casinos do not make someone a gambling addict. We must have a susceptibility to addiction, which arises from the pain of not liking who we believe we are, a state brought on by a pre-existing vulnerability from an environment of stress.

The human brain develops roughly 25 percent in the womb and 75 percent after birth. By age three, the most significant brain growth portion, up to 90 percent, is established.[7] The remaining 10 percent continues into the early twenties.

A child must have good nutrition, physical security, and consistent emotional nurturing for the brain to complete its critical wiring. Even a single traumatic

> "A radically different notion has replaced the view that genes play a decisive role in the way a person's brain develops: the expression of genetic potentials is, for the most part, contingent on the environment."
> ~Dr. Gabor Maté, physician, addiction and trauma expert, author

incident can block this essential growth and cause a child to turn inward and lose touch with who they are.

The undeveloped brain, incapable of understanding trauma, neglect, abuse, or emotional loss, will most likely make a child believe the abuse is their fault, and their mistaken identity begins. In these cases, it's likely that the child won't develop the necessary emotional wiring to handle and enjoy life.

The bottom line is if we grew up with stressed-out parents, we were prone to being stressed children, no matter how much our parents loved us and strived to do their best.

∞

The Beginning of My Mistaken Identity

There was unrelenting tension in my home, walking on eggshells between episodes of abuse. As a child, I couldn't name the cause or explain its results. I only knew I was uncomfortable, afraid, and wanted it to end.

I hid under my bed when I was a little boy trying to avoid Dad coming home drunk. One time he pulled me into the living room, "playfully" bending and twisting my baby finger, demanding that I say uncle as I sobbed and begged him to stop. He would laugh at my suffering. He also doled out similar humiliations, shaming me in front of others under the guise of "just playing." The message to never show sensitivity or vulnerability or make a mistake planted and cultivated the seeds of pain and my mistaken identity.

In contrast, my mother and I had an unhealthy relationship where we kept secrets from the rest of the family, and I felt responsible for her emotional well-being. I felt pulled in two different directions; the fear of Dad and an unhealthy attachment to Mom. I escaped to my best friend's house whenever I could.

Whenever my Dad and I had problems, Mom told me that he was under a lot of stress and that Dad loved me, but I wanted her to stop his behavior. The unspoken message was that I didn't matter. My addiction was initially an effective way to silence the painful voice inside me that relentlessly reinforced that message.

People often say that their parents did the best they could. They don't say as often that healing and forgiveness take truth and time. I now understand that my parents didn't cause my addiction at all, that they too had their own unhealed trauma.

∞

Multigenerational Trauma

Creating a genogram in treatment set me on the path of healing and forgiveness. Much like a family tree, the genogram is a graphic chart of generational addictions, traumas, and secrets. My mother's lineage had heavy drinkers and alcoholics many generations deep. In contrast, my father's side had heavy drinkers and an abusive mother who, according to his sisters, should never have had children. Grandmother always treated me well, but I intuitively knew not to piss her off.

27

My grandfather fought in World War II, leaving his wife to raise the children alone. My father didn't see his father until he was four years old. My aunt told me that she vividly remembered beatings with coat hangers, broomsticks, and hairbrushes. She could not recall her mom hugging her until she was seven. She also said that her mother deliberately burned my father's hand with a cigarette.

∞

Trauma

Understanding what trauma isn't is the way to know what it is. Trauma is *not* when there is sexual, physical, or emotional abuse. It's

> "Trauma is not what happens to you, but what happens inside you as a result of what happens to you."
> ~Dr. Gabor Maté, physician, addiction and trauma expert

not the suicide of a loved one, absent caregivers, neglected babies, or when a soldier is shot. Trauma is the *aftermath* of the event—how an individual internally processes the event.

Adults often think that extreme events are the only form of trauma. They forget that painful, stressful events that may seem minor to them can be significant to infants, toddlers, children, and adolescents. They have the potential to harm their sense of self, their relationships, and how they see the world as teenagers and adults. It's like wearing dirty glasses that distort reality. The more traumatized we are, the more limited our potential for critical thinking, curiosity, emotional intelligence, and loving relationships.

Acknowledging, feeling, and accepting the pain in our bodies are the first steps to our healing. There is no other way.

∞

Children under the age of three usually won't remember details of their abuse, but their bodies and unconscious mind will. This memory is called *implicit memory*.

They feel *confused* and unsafe without knowing why. Unless we address the emotional aftermath of trauma in a timely fashion,

> Few adults can remember anything before the age of three. A recent study documents that earliest memories begin to fade roughly at age seven, a phenomenon known as childhood amnesia.[8]

it will continue to live in the body. As it's said in the yoga world, "Our issues live in our tissues."

The opposite is called *explicit memory*. Our conscious, intentional recollection of factual information, previous experiences, and concepts. Explicit memory can be divided into two categories: *episodic memory*, which stores specific personal experiences, and *semantic memory*, which stores factual information.

Remember this the next time you judge a drug-addicted sex worker, homeless person, or criminal because they were most likely traumatized as a child. We need to have the same amount of compassion for them as we do for the abused children we see in news reports. They are the same people all grown up.

Other sources of trauma can occur after we leave our family of origin. For instance, I have friends in recovery who have experienced traumatic events such as being raped, stabbed, and shot.

> "Eighty percent of women with substance abuse have suffered sexual abuse, and two out of three of substance users report abuse as children."[9]
> ~Jane Liebschutz, et al., *Journal of Substance Abuse Treatment*

I found a friend after he committed suicide in his jail cell. The impact of any trauma feeds the mistaken identity. The more we avoid dealing with trauma, the worse our addiction becomes.

∞

The Trauma of Marlboro Man

Almost twenty years ago, I met 28-year-old Jim (not his real name) while I was in treatment for the second time. He looked like the Marlboro man from the cigarette ad campaign that ran from 1954 to 1999. He dressed the part in a perfect mustache, cowboy boots, tight Wrangler jeans, and cool ball caps. All the clients at the center called him Marlboro Man. Something else about Jim's appearance was baffling—a visible bulge in his jeans that many of us made fun of behind his back. One day, Jim shared the following secret he'd held inside for many years.

Jim grew up in a wealthy family in which both parents worked. As a preschooler, he was looked after by the next-door neighbor during the day. Unfortunately, the neighbor didn't do her job. No one knew that her kids would take little Jimmy into the basement, duct tape his mouth, perform sexual acts, then lock him in the closet. This abuse went on for two years, and it changed Jim. He admitted that he stuffed his pants with a banana or socks because other men wouldn't think he was gay or weak and try to take advantage of him. It was no wonder that Jim sought drugs and alcohol to numb the pain.

Jim's healing moment came when he could share his toxic shame in a safe place with compassionate people. It always amazes me how our walls and judgments come down once we hear another person's story.

∞

The Difference Between Pain and Suffering

Pain is a physical and emotional experience within our body that serves as an alert. On the other hand, suffering is how we perceive and interpret the pain from our thoughts, judgments, and beliefs.

Our suffering is the disconnection of the mind and body. It turns pain into hell, and the more we are disconnected, the more we suffer.

Inevitably, we will all endure physical, emotional, mental pain and suffering, sickness, stress, injury, fatigue, decline, and, eventually,

> "It isn't what happens to us that causes us to suffer; it's what we say to ourselves about what happens."
> ~Pema Chodron, American Tibetan Buddhist nun, teacher

death. While our fearful brain will try to convince us to escape, we are neither the thoughts of our brain or the pain. We are spiritual beings of Light—timeless and powerful beyond measure.

Psychiatrist Viktor Frankl's powerful memoir *Man's Search for Meaning* describes his spiritual survival while in Nazi death camps. Frankl's experience taught him that when dealing with his suffering he always had a choice in his response. This understanding helped him move forward with renewed purpose. We all have this same freedom.

I had to stop using my addiction to escape pain and face myself. I only found recovery and meaning in my life when I chose to make use of my painful past experiences to help others. My worst nightmare became my greatest gift.

∞

One Coin, Two Sides

Most people believe that pain is bad and pleasure is good, but the two are inseparable, like night and day, birth and death. If one cannot exist without the other, how can one be good and the other bad? When we call pleasure good or pain bad, we make it easier to attach our identity to them. If we want a life that is 100 percent painless, then we will have to live a life that is 100 percent without pleasure as well—an impossibility.

31

Addiction is about trying to flip the coin of pain to pleasure by using our substance or behavior of choice. However, the more we seek peaks of pleasure, the more profound the valleys of despair as we get caught up in an addictive cycle. When we try to escape pain, we make it worse because "what we resist persists." It is vital to understand that we have no control over when the coin flips.

We must trust that pain will return to pleasure when it's time. We have no control over when that happens. What we can control is how we respond to the pain.

∞

Pain Is Not Our Enemy

When we stop running and face our pain and suffering, we will see them as signs to direct us back onto the path

> Learn more by viewing the video, Learn to Suffer Well.
> https://youtu.be/sVgsc9m5XOw

of Truth and Love. By becoming a conscious observer, we can acknowledge that it's okay to be in pain, but pain is not who we are and has nothing to do with our true nature. Pain is a feeling, and like any other feeling, it comes and goes.

If you want to rewrite your story, wake up! Being in the now is what we need, not more stories. The beautiful thing about life is that good can come out of pain and suffering. It's in our overcoming that we rise above where we once were and find depths of love we never thought possible.

∞

A Declaration of Commitment to Truth, Love, and Peace

"Pain is not who I am. I am the essence of Love."

LAYER THREE

TOXIC SHAME

The reason behind relapse is most often toxic shame.

For more than fourteen years, many members of the twelve-step fellowship knew me as the relapse king. I would be clean for thirty days, then relapse; ninety days, then relapse; six months, then relapse; eleven months, then relapse. Wash, rinse, repeat.

I hit bottom after bottom. I completed programs at seven treatment centers, relapsing after each one. I worked through the twelve steps three times with sponsors, writing a searching moral inventory (step four), and sharing it with my sponsor (step five), only to relapse shortly afterward each time.

Over and over again, my mind chanted this paragraph from *Alcoholics Anonymous*: "Rarely have we seen a person fail who has thoroughly followed our path. Those who do not recover are people who cannot or will not completely give themselves to this simple program, usually men and women who are constitutionally incapable of being honest with themselves. There are such unfortunates."

I came to believe I was one of those unfortunates. My toxic shame whispered that I was unworthy, not enough, a loser who would never recover. Believing I was flawed and defective, I caused untold damage to myself as I used different guises to try to get

33

others to love me because I did not love myself. It's no wonder I could not stop the relentless cycle of relapse.

For sustainable recovery, toxic shame and its hurtful messages must be reprogramed with awareness, great compassion, and repetition.

I consider John Bradshaw, the first to name shame as a major component of addiction, an enormous recovery influence. His book, *Healing the Shame that Binds You,* was instrumental in eventually undoing my constant relapses and serial people-pleasing.

> "Hell, in my opinion, is never finding your true self and never living your own life or knowing who you are. This is the fate that lies at the end of the journey of ever-deepening toxic shame."[10]
> ~John Bradshaw, educator, counselor, motivational speaker, author

∞

People-Pleasing

My premise about pleasing others was that agreeing to everything was selfless and honorable, that I didn't want to hurt anyone's feelings. In reality, it was about me and my inability to confront my feelings of inferiority.

It took a long time to figure out that my people-pleasing attracted takers and left me feeling like a victim again. All I needed

> To embody the Divine, to be one with Love, we have to put ourselves first. When flying, we must first put on our oxygen mask before helping anyone else.

was to be accepted for myself. In my final years of addiction, I became a taker just as much as a people pleaser. I was a hostage to my mistaken identity.

∞

The Missing "Something"

My false belief was that men must always be strong and never share their thoughts and feelings. I believed that rejection, criticism, and abandonment would destroy me. The consequences of appearing vulnerable were too big a risk to take.

I had to be willing to do things differently. If I continued repeating the same patterns—the same shit, over and over—I would continue to struggle and fail to find lasting recovery. That something different was vulnerability.

I had to honestly share *all* my dark secrets and insecurities with a few compassionate, nonjudgmental people or continue to live in misery. It was that simple and that difficult.

> "It is in our vulnerability that our true power resides. If you want to be more powerful in your own life, let your vulnerability show!"
> ~Liz McDougall

After doing so, I recognized that being vulnerable is the most courageous act of self-love. The more vulnerable I became, the more I was transformed and healed from the inside out. The toxic shame began to melt away.

∞

The Antidotes to Toxic Shame

The roots of toxic shame usually begin in a hostile environment where sexual, physical, or emotional abuse harms our inner voice. The effects of this shame can continue through generations.

Toxic shame and healthy shame are different. Toxic shame looks inward, focusing on who we are, not something we did. Toxic shame says, "I *am* a mistake." Healthy shame says, "I *made* a mistake." My toxic shame was fed by

> The enemy of shame is the understanding and awareness of its origin.

35

an inability to see that human imperfections, shortcomings, fallibilities, vulnerabilities, sensitivity, and making mistakes are all a part of being human, not a life sentence of shame.

It was crucial to share my vulnerability with other men. Why? Because I decided never to trust another man once I left home at 19.

We must do the critical work of dissecting our toxic shame to understand and repair the faulty programming from childhood that we had accepted as truth. We must rewire these long-held false and limiting beliefs or continue to hate who we think we are.

> "Toxic shame is soul murder."
> ~Anonymous

When my face becomes hot and flushed, and my pulse increases, I recognize and acknowledge shame,

> Learn more from my video, No More Shame.
> https://youtu.be/0Kt2vAFpfSU

then share my experience with a compassionate person I trust. Shame cannot survive when shared.

∞

The Shadow Self

Our shadow lives within our mistaken identity as shameful, unacceptable, annoying, disgusting, or horrifying secrets about ourselves that we try to hide from our self and others. As the recovery slogan says, "We are as sick as our secrets."

Trying to control the shadows created by unhealed trauma and toxic shame is like trying to hold

> "Our shadow is the person that we would rather not be."
> ~Carl Jung, psychologist, psychiatrist, founder of analytic psychology

many big beach balls under the water. One by one, they will pop up in times of stress and anger. It's only when we gently and courageously shine light, without self-deception or illusion, onto our shadow that we will have the courage to embrace ourselves and acknowledge our full humanity. We must honor and accept our shadow self, understanding:

- All humans need both darkness and light to be authentic.
- Within the so-called darkness, often unacknowledged and unrecognized, are our most significant gifts.
- Our shadow is here to teach us how to love more, not less.
- When we judge or project another person's shadow, it is most likely or once was ours.

∞

The Masks of the Shadow

We use masks to hide our thoughts and feelings and to present what we believe to be an acceptable version of ourselves. The overachiever, the clown, the rescuer, the intellectual, the gangster, and others are among the masks we may use.

Pretending I was easygoing and self-assured was the first mask I'd wear whenever I met someone new. If I felt I wasn't receiving the respect I was looking for, I would switch to my charmer mask. If that failed, I would wear a passive mask of belligerence to reject people before they could do the same to me. My masks were all about seeking acceptance from others because I couldn't find it for myself. I believed I wasn't good enough.

We consciously or unconsciously create social masks to protect ourselves from perceived danger. But the reality is that these masks destroy our lives by keeping us from our true essence.

∞

Rejection

The fear of rejection and pretending rejection didn't bother me was my most prevalent shadow, which caused many relapses. My reaction to rejection was never about what happened, but my perceptions and interpretations of what happened. In other words, rejection triggered my false and limiting beliefs about myself. We have no choice because the unconscious mind will automatically trigger our suppressed pain (trauma) until it's brought into consciousness and healed at the body level.

To those who suffer from toxic shame, rejection can feel like death because we take it personally. Ironically, this mindset only increases the likelihood of others rejecting us.

In reality, the fear of rejection was originally wired into humanity when we could die from rejection. For example, if I lived back in tribal times and didn't conform, banishment into the harsh environment would lead to starvation. Belonging is a fundamental need; just like food and water, we need others. When I recognized rejection as the old wiring of primitive fear, it lost its power and opened me up to new perceptions:

- Whenever I perceive rejection, I understand that it is not an attack on me personally. I know it is just past programming.
- Rejection is a perception (not a feeling) that causes pain in the body. It needs to be healed in the body, not just the mind. I had to feel the pain in the body. Remember, we can't let go—what we can't first let in.
- Our thoughts may tell us that rejection is evidence that we are unworthy. The truth is that we are never rejected.
- The hurt from rejection is a valid and painful human experience and nothing to be ashamed of.

- Think of rejection as a redirection. Two examples: we may experience a devastating divorce only to find our true love a year later. We may lose our job and then land one of our dreams.

∞

A Declaration of Commitment to Truth, Love, and Peace

"I release all unexpressed and unresolved toxic shame. I will instead practice honesty, vulnerability, and courage."

LAYER FOUR

RECOVERY MYTHS

꒳⊙ ⊙꒳

*Believing a myth can propel a counterproductive course
of action, or it may discourage any action at all.*

꒳⊙ ⊙꒳

The pervasive myth in popular culture and among professionals
is that someone with an addiction cannot recover until they
experience enough pain, a.k.a. hit a rock bottom that will give
them the willingness to ask for and accept help.

I'd hit numerous rock bottoms over twenty years in active
addiction, each worse than the last. I had willingly gone to
treatment and followed their directions seven times. Neither the
ever-deepening humiliation of a rock bottom nor my sincere
willingness helped me get sober.

My real motivation for
wanting the rock-bottom
myth to be true was
simple. It was the place
where I would magically
never use again without
having to do the work of
recovery.

> "My clients don't hit bottom; they
> live on the bottom. The bottom is
> not new for them."
>   ~William L. White, addiction
>   recovery and policy author,
>   Lighthouse Institute founder

∞

Bottomless

The voices of well-meaning friends, family, and society combined within my mind to ask if I'd had enough pain to stop. As a person with an addiction who could not stop, I felt I needed to continue to use until I hit my ultimate rock bottom. As the consequences of using got worse and worse, I wondered if I was bottomless.

2005

I was eleven months clean, living in a comfortable, fully furnished downtown apartment in a good neighborhood, attending meetings regularly, doing step work, and had a great sponsor. I had adopted Tiny, a puppy I cherished, and was dating Linda, who lived next door.

I felt my recovery program was solid, but ten days before my one-year sobriety date, I hit the pipe again, convincing Linda and myself that it was just a slip. Reassured that I was okay, Linda, with plans to visit family out of town, gave me the keys to her apartment so I could water her plants.

Seven days into my relapse, I was neglecting Tiny, had sold my TV, computer, and camera, then stole Linda's TV, laptop, and camera to buy more rock. Disgusted with myself, I called the cops and left a message on Linda's voicemail, telling them what I had done. The next morning, two Toronto police officers arrested me and called animal protection to take Tiny away. I spent the next three months in jail worrying about Tiny and Linda. I would never see either of them again. Wasn't this, finally, rock bottom?

Out of all the things I had done in addiction years, this failure brought the most shame. I kept it secret and suffered for over ten years. My treatment of Linda was awful, but abandoning Tiny felt unforgivable.

∞

Myths help us make sense of the world. To understand addiction, a disease that makes no sense, people developed the rock bottom myth. Is there any other disease or condition where physicians and other professionals believe their patients need more pain and suffering before they can recover?

"What would you think of a doctor who told a cancer patient that treatment of any kind would be a waste of time because the disease is not yet critical? Any intervention at this point would interfere with a process that will, in time, produce lots of pain, degradation, and maybe irreparable physical damage. Oh, sure, early intervention might save you the need to have your arm amputated but losing an arm might be what it takes to change your attitude and make you receptive to treatment.

"No matter how insane this approach would be—should I say evil?—it is precisely how the system has traditionally dealt with addictions. With no other medical condition—not even mental illness or neurosis—is the governing idea that the disease must be allowed to cause a great deal of damage to prepare someone for help.

"For that matter, with no other medical condition is failure of treatment consistently blamed on the patient."[11]

~Dr. Peter Ferentzy, addiction scientist and author

We need to eradicate this fear-based harmful philosophy. Lasting recovery begins when our focus shifts from the problem to the solution found in the work of recovery. I

"Research has shown that even the addicts forced into treatment—perhaps by a court—have the same chance of getting and staying sober as anyone else."

~Dr. Nora Volkow, director of the National Institute on Drug Abuse

didn't have to hit rock bottom to recover. I needed an awakening of consciousness.

Can We Help the Unwilling?

When an unwilling person with an addiction is at a support group or treatment center, they will often hear others' experiences that mirror their own. It can give them clarity that may provide them with the willingness to accept their problem and find the solution. I believe mirroring can affect the unwilling, even after one meeting. Magic can happen!

Simultaneously, research shows that it is dangerous and harmful to force someone into recovery who is unwilling. More concrete research needs to be done on this critical topic. Regardless, it is essential to never shame anyone into seeking help. What is required is compassion.

Recovery expert Rich Jones also challenges these myths. "No research supports the legitimacy of hitting bottom as a helpful construct, at least in terms of outcomes," he writes and continues,

> ... The necessity of willingness as a prerequisite for successful treatment has been entirely deconstructed by *motivational interviewing*. The concept of hitting bottom has never been established as a legitimate therapeutic approach, yet counselors, therapists, and programs offer that advice thousands of times a day. There is something tragic about it guiding our nation's healthcare response to addiction.

> ... The idea of willingness fits in a fractured and largely ineffective treatment system. The industry sees relapse after treatment as a lack of willingness on the part of the patient—the person didn't get better because they didn't want to get better. This places blame on the patient ... we need to develop new and creative ways of treating people.

... Ten years from now, the addiction treatment and recovery industry will not resemble what we have today. The transition has already begun. I thank Paul Noiles for the opportunity to contribute to this important work. I believe Paul reflects this new way of thinking.

Thanks, Rich Jones! You can find his full article at the back of the book.

∞

In *Dealing with Addiction: Why the 20th Century Was Wrong,* Dr. Ferentzy, a researcher, shares the three predictors of recovery success: social support through stable connections with family and friends; social standing with housing, work, financial means, and ties to mainstream society; and cognitive functioning, the brain-based skills to carry out tasks. Think about it. How much more difficult would it be to find lasting recovery without emotional support from family and friends, a job, housing, or a sense of belonging?

We need to connect with others who mirror back love, help us see our blind spots, and support us.

> It's one of life's many paradoxes: no one can save us, yet we need connection with other people.

∞

The Unmovable Rock Bottom

Hitting bottom as a necessity for recovery is a generally accepted premise both inside and outside recovery programs, but hitting bottom is not necessary! Even AA's *Twelve Steps and Twelve Traditions* says the bottom can be raised, a way of saying that rock bottom is not necessary. While hitting bottom does not guarantee we will stop using, it means we have come to the realization we can't do it alone. We admit our powerlessness.

Here is what some other people in recovery have to say about rock bottom: "Not a final state of affairs, but a temporary opportunity …" "I think what is required is humility. I have seen many people recover from alcoholism without hitting rock bottom …" "Losing hope, self-respect, and dignity—rather than jobs or houses—brought me to my knees and took me to a desperate enough place where I was willing to listen …" "I called it a pinnacle, a place where I could see with clarity that I was either going to die or get help."

While hitting rock bottom may have been the end of your addiction, recovery does not depend on it. As it's said in the rooms, "Take what you like and leave the rest."

∞

I later realized that I had been judging my recovery based on others' professional and personal opinions—I identified relapse as a failure and unbroken clean time as a success.

I'm eternally grateful that my mentors, Reverend Lorraine and Reverend Darrell, had different perspectives. They saw me as a miracle in progress, a man who, after each relapse, continued on the path to recovery and spiritual growth.

> A person with a nicotine addiction generally makes eight attempts before quitting. Each time he is encouraged not to stop trying. Shouldn't a person with cocaine, meth, heroin, alcohol, or any other addiction receive the same understanding and compassion?

The truth is that every human being is in a state of recovery. It's part of the human condition to release the ill-informed belief in ego and a separate self.

∞

A Declaration of Commitment to Truth, Love, and Peace

"I don't need to hit rock bottom to recover. I will surrender, engage in the work of recovery, and find my freedom."

LAYER FIVE

THE MIND

I am not my mind.

Thinking of ourselves is the core of every addiction; we are addicted to thinking. The compulsively redefining, improving, and perfecting our personal story is the mental prison of "me, myself, and I."

While not every thought is negative, it is the compulsive, disempowering, repetitive thoughts that wreak havoc in our lives. And make no mistake, it's the past unhealed trauma that causes the most damage in our minds.

> *Experts say we have a little less than one thought every second. There are 86,000 seconds in a day.*

∞

Homeless in 1998

While wandering around a used bookstore in Toronto, I accidentally knocked over a stack of books. I placed them all back on the table except one. For some reason, I was drawn to *The Power of Now* by Eckhart Tolle. I opened the book to chapter one, "You Are Not Your Mind." I was floored and said to myself, "Get the fuck out of here!" But something inside me asked if he might have been correct. It gave me great hope because my substance use directly responded to the pain of never-ending negative thoughts.

I stole Tolle's book and read every word like it was food from the heavens. My road to awakening and recovery truly began then.

Hijacked by the belief that my negative thoughts were who I was, it's no wonder I hated myself and kept relapsing.

After studying Tolle, I realized that I had equated my thoughts (thinking) with who I was (being) from early childhood. I learned from Tolle that my thoughts had nothing

> "There is nothing more important to true growth than realizing that you are not the voice of the mind—you are the one who hears it."[12]
> ~Michael A. Singer, author, Temple of the Universe founder

to do with who I am. It was another big light bulb moment—*I was the consciousness that had thoughts, not the thoughts themselves.*

1999

Addict-Man

While I was in treatment at Stonehenge Therapeutic Community, I met Bret, my brother from another mother, who described the voice of his addiction as "addict-man." According to Bret, addict-man was the little bastard sitting on his shoulder, whispering in his ear, controlling every move he made. Within a short time, everyone in the center was using addict-man to talk about our addictions. It became a compassionate and funny way to separate the addiction from our true selves. I intuitively knew that Bret was onto something, and one day, I would write about addict-man. I need to acknowledge Bret for his contribution and the friendship we still have.

∞

In *The Power of Now*, Eckhart Tolle writes about thinking, "I cannot live with myself any longer," and getting ready for suicide. Fortunately, his next thought was, how could there be an "I" who cannot live with "myself?" Tolle would realize that only one of them could be real. In essence, it was no different from what Bret, and the rest of us, experienced when we described the voice of Addict-Man. Like Tolle, I would eventually discover the real me (Love/Spirit/Being) and the false me (mistaken identity).

It was through the practice of daily meditation, mindfulness, and observing the present moment that I learned to slow down the many addict-man thoughts. And in the process, I realized that I was not my thoughts, only the conscious observer of them.

∞

The Observer

Until I learned how to be the observer, not the judge, juror, and executioner of my thoughts, I

> *I was not my mind but the watcher of my mind.*

had no long-term relief. Learning to observe allowed me to see my hijacked mind from a different perspective.

From there, I could see my thoughts and actions from a higher state of awakened consciousness and eventually stop repeating the same patterns. When our perception of reality changes, we change.

I was finally able to break the stronghold of toxic shame I had been carrying around since I was a little boy. I was able to stop the voice of "I am not good enough." By observing without trying to change anything, everything changed for me.

> "Through our eyes, the universe is perceiving itself. Through our ears, the universe is listening to its harmonies. We are the witnesses through which the universe becomes conscious of its glory, of its magnificence."
> -Alan Watts, author, speaker

That "I" am the observer of my thoughts remains the most important discovery in my awakening journey, one that allows me to see truth more objectively and find compassion for myself.

Try it yourself. Sit quietly for a moment and observe the currents of thought traveling through your mind, like water flowing down a river or clouds passing in the sky. If a thought comes, don't stop it. If it doesn't, don't force it. You are merely an observer. This is the essence of mindfulness meditation. The more we practice observing our thoughts, the more we realize they are often only the meaningless chatter of the "monkey mind."

Shortly after his enlightenment, Buddha was seated under a tree in meditation when the Brahmin Dona approached and asked:

"Sir, will you be a god?"

"No, Brahmin."

"Sir, will you be a heavenly angel?"

"No, Brahmin."

"Sir, will you be a demon?"

"No, Brahmin."

"Sir, will you be a human being?"

"No, Brahmin."

"Then, Sir, what indeed will you be?"

Buddha replied, "Brahmin, whatever defilements there be owing to the presence of which a person may be identified as a god or a heavenly angel or a demon or a human being, all these defilements in me are abandoned, cut off at the root, made like a palm-tree stump, done away with, and are no more subject to future arising.

"Just as, Brahmin, a blue or red or white lotus born in water, grows in water and stands up above the water untouched by it, so too I, who was born in the world and grew up in the world, have transcended the world, and I live untouched by the world. Remember me as one who is enlightened [awake]."

Buddha understood that everything beyond "I am awake" is temporary. The mind, with its cravings, thoughts, and feelings, the body, material possessions, fears, and even beliefs have no permanence. Most of our suffering will end when we recognize that our attachment to our thoughts, emotions, and body sensations is the root of suffering. Our awakened consciousness is eternal.

Had I not stumbled across understanding that I was not my mind—what I now call the Holy Grail of recovery—chances are I would still be relapsing or dead.

∞

A Declaration of Commitment to Truth, Love, and Peace

"I am not my mind. I am the consciousness that experiences thoughts, feelings, and body sensations. There is no permanence in the mind, only constant change."

LAYER SIX

EMOTIONS AND FEELINGS

꾀 ⊚

*I used for one reason: I couldn't handle my
emotions because I equated feelings with who I was.*

꾀 ⊚

Feelings are the mind/body response to emotions. When we resist or suppress our feelings, we disconnect from our truth, and suffering follows. Addiction is a sure way to cope with our feelings, but eventually, even that stops working.

When I entered recovery, I began to see many other coping mechanisms I developed—blaming, victimhood, intimidation, silence, hypervigilance, risky behavior, anger, hate, and avoidance, to name but a few. Most of them began in childhood as a way to survive. They were an unconscious way of not dealing with my feelings in the present moment.

This knowledge helped undo my toxic shame and practice compassion whenever triggered, rather than reacting with a coping mechanism. With my mentor's guidance, I was finally able to face, feel, and heal my past wounds in a healthy way.

∞

Lessons I learned:

1. The way we deal with our feelings will determine the course of our life.

2. We must take responsibility for all our feelings and let go of our perceptions (stories). Stories don't heal us; feelings do.

3. There are neither good (right) or bad (wrong) feelings. Identifying them as good or bad sets us up to resist them. We need all our emotions and their duality to experience the fullness of life.

4. Recognize that anger, disgust, sadness, and hate are road signs that reveal our need to learn, heal, and grow. Accept all your feelings. You'll find they are treasures.

5. Be the observer of your feelings, not the judge, jury, or executioner.

∞

Here is an example of a story I repressed and told no one. It continued to live in my pain body until I shared it with my mentor as an adult. Only then did I let in the painful emotions and safely let them go.

Dad won the golf tournament with me as his caddy. He celebrated his win at the bar as I, a twelve-year-old, waited nervously in the car, hoping he wouldn't return drunk. A couple of hours later, he showed up wasted. I was terrified about the forty-minute drive ahead of us. Each time he started to doze at the wheel, I had to shake and yell at him. As he swerved on the road, I had to clutch and redirect the steering wheel to keep us from hitting traffic head-on. I felt somewhat relieved when we finally made it safely into the city. At the last stoplight, Dad passed out. No matter how I tried, he wouldn't wake up. As I sobbed, I somehow figured out how to drive the rest of the way home and park the car. I didn't tell anyone because I was afraid Dad would hurt me for telling. I developed the belief that my feelings or I, didn't matter.

∞

Early Development

Developing healthy emotional integration ideally begins in childhood. I learned early on in my family of origin that expressing my emotions was unacceptable, and if I did, I could get hurt. My self-worth plunged each time I thought my emotions were invalid or unimportant. I began to suppress my feelings to protect myself.

By the time I was an adult, I was hardwired to attach my identity to painful experiences. Unable to recognize my true feelings and

> *We spend our childhood wanting to grow up and spend our adulthood trying to undo our childhood without knowing it.*

their changing nature, I continued to deny and manipulate my emotions. My inability to know my true feelings eventually led to two suicide attempts.

2004

While living in a basement apartment, I put a rope around my neck, attached it to a light fixture in the ceiling, stood on a chair, then kicked the chair away. Ten seconds later, the ceiling caved in. The owners, who lived upstairs, rushed down, opened the door with their key, and called 911. I went to the hospital. There was an eviction notice on my door when I returned.

2005

After collecting enough pills to kill myself, I went on a last cocaine binge. When my money ran out, I went home and swallowed all the pills. A short time later, I passed out, crashing on and shattering the glass table in my living room. My

> *There are no lost souls. Whether for seconds or a century, all souls are Love.*

upstairs neighbors heard the crash and called 911. I was rushed to the hospital, then discharged six hours later. I had a needle in my arm a short time after that.

I should have died countless times during my addiction years, but somehow I didn't. Why do some people die from addiction, and others do not? No one knows, and any attempt to answer would be insensitive to those who have lost loved ones. I see no such thing as a wasted life. It's a real miracle that we are even born; according to probability, it's about 1 in 400 trillion. We are all miracles of Life.

∞

Ownership/Awareness

Treatment centers tell residents to "own their feelings." However, when we take ownership of our feelings, especially with mistaken identity, we risk increasing our toxic shame and chance of relapse. I will clarify; *awareness* of our feelings, not ownership of them, is the key.

Being told at seven treatment centers that I needed to "own my feelings" quickly led me to relapse after I left treatment because I saw my negative feelings as my identity. I know I'm not alone in this. We need to know that *we are the consciousness that has feelings, not the feelings themselves.* I began to recover once I let go of ownership of my feelings and replaced it with self-awareness.

> "Feelings come and go like clouds in a windy sky. Conscious breathing is my anchor."
> -Thich Nhat Hanh, Zen master, writer, poet, scholar, peacemaker

The healthiest people on the planet are those with self-awareness. They can feel their feelings without

> "Feelings are just visits. Let them come and go."
> ~ Mooji, spiritual teacher

guilt, shame, or judgment. Feelings are just energy. They are part of our experience.

We develop freedom by validating and honoring all feelings without judgment, resistance, or ownership. The key is to embrace any unpleasant feeling, name it, and with practice, learn to locate it. Where are your feelings in your body? Is fear churning in your stomach, a tightness in your chest, rapid heartbeat? Is sadness a constriction in your throat? *Naming and embracing these feelings is a way to find that they are not the monsters we thought they were.* With practice, I changed my relationship with my feelings by not being attached to or basing my identity on them. Learning to disidentify with my feelings was pivotal to my recovery from addiction.

∞

Move the Energy

Whenever I wasn't feeling emotionally well, Reverend Lorraine would suggest that it was most likely the result of being on the hamster wheel of compulsive thinking. "Move the energy!" she'd advise. To break the stronghold of rethinking painful thoughts and return to a healthy balance of body, spirit, and mind, we must remember that everything is energy. Connecting with others and engaging in arts, crafts, music, exercise, and meditation are just a few ways to move energy. Find what works for you. When I feel an overwhelming amount of anger and can't figure out why, I hit the gym; halfway through the workout, my answer naturally comes to me because I am not in my head.

When I'm feeling stuck in heavy emotions, I call my mentor or sponsor or one of my closest friends in recovery. Shining light on my emotions

> Learn more about Emotional Pain: How to Deal with It.
> https://youtu.be/wCwLoPnxwRcc

with someone else gives me a different perspective and releases some power of those emotions.

The Blame Game

No longer blaming others for any of my feelings and accepting personal responsibility for my emotional health was one of the best things I've ever done. I now rarely say, "You made me angry," or "You made me sad." Our serenity level depends on losing blame and recognizing the power of taking responsibility for our emotional health.

No one can make us feel how we feel. It happens through our perceptions and interpretations in the moment to moment. When we know this, we're less likely to blame and more likely to move to the solution of looking at ourselves quickly.

> "Light and darkness happen within you; pain and pleasure happen within you; joy and misery happen within you. Everything that has ever happened to you has happened within yourself! The events around you may not be determined by you, but how your experience of life is on this planet is 100% determined by you."
>
> -Sadhguru, Indian yogi and author

Sadhguru hit the nail on the head—how we experience life is up to us.

∞

A Declaration of Commitment to Truth, Love, and Peace

"I honor all feelings, knowing that no feeling defines me. No feeling is permanent."

LAYER SEVEN

BELIEFS

We won't find our authentic self until
we recognize and undo our false, limiting beliefs.

Conflicting beliefs—"My belief is right, and yours is wrong"is the cause of much chaos in the world. Beliefs are destroying the fabric of life itself. Beliefs are not facts or truth, no matter how passionately proclaimed. Beliefs are ways of thinking, acts of consciousness that are the fundamental building blocks that create our perceived reality. In contrast to a thought, a belief is an assumed truth designed to deal with fear.

∞

Most of Our Beliefs Are Not Ours

Beliefs are generally formed in two ways: by our experiences or by accepting what others tell us to be true. We learn most of our hard-wired beliefs from our parents and extended relationships as children. Family, friends, teachers, religious figures, culture, and society help program our belief system with their rules, values, religion, and much more. These beliefs end up telling us who to be, what to do, and how to live.

Consequently, two people's belief systems can create different perceptions of the same life event. Share a family experience with your siblings about your upbringing, and you'll see how each remembers it differently.

Questioning the beliefs of those in authority was taboo for most of us. If we did, rejection, withholding of love, intimidation, shame, or violence could follow.

> "Seeing is not believing. Believing is seeing! You see things, not as they are, but as you are."
> ~Eric Butterworth, minister, author, radio personality

These are control mechanisms, and control is about power, not love.

We fearfully assimilate other people's beliefs as a way to protect ourselves, even when our intuition tells us their beliefs are wrong.

> "As long as the mind clings to belief, it is held in a prison."
> ~Jiddu Krishnamurti, philosopher, writer, speaker

We subconsciously begin to build our mistaken identity to make sense of our experiences and fit in.

The way out of our prison is to investigate, identify, and delete the outdated programming, rules, and beliefs that hold us back from knowing our authentic self. It doesn't require new beliefs; intelligence, remaining open, and truth-seeking is all we need. If not, we continue the unthinkable behavior and consequences of addiction.

> Truth belongs to everyone.

Consequences

In 2001, I desperately returned to Ottawa, the city where I'd found phenomenal success in the 1980s. However, this time, my home was the Salvation Army. It was another failed geographical move as I continued to shoplift and use my substance of choice daily.

As I walked down the street on my way to the "fence," the middleman who would buy the merchandise I'd stolen from the local mall, three gangbangers approached. Intuitively, I put my hands around the handles of my backpack and stopped to chat. As we talked, one of the guys took a brick from behind his back and walloped me so hard that I heard my bones break. I ran down the street as they chased me. After I got away, I looked into a truck's side-view mirror, where I saw that the left side of my face caved in, completely gone. It didn't matter because it wouldn't stop me from getting high. I sold the stolen merchandise, got my drugs, and used, all with a collapsed face. Hours later, I made it back to my cot at the Salvation Army, where a staff member shone a bright flashlight on my face, then called 911. An ambulance rushed me to the emergency room. A doctor performed plastic surgery to repair my broken cheekbone in two places and the orbital bones around my eye in nine.

It's easy now to see how my long-held false beliefs about myself were the real reasons I continued having many near-death consequences. You see, there was a part of me, the part that lived in the subconscious mind, that wanted me to die.

∞

The Subconscious Mind

The subconscious mind is like a super-computer with preloaded programs of unintentional and habitual thoughts, behaviors, and plans running in the background. Its job is to create reality out of its programs and prove the applications correct. The subconscious mind processes 40 million bits of data every second, the conscious mind only about 40 bits of data per second, making the subconscious mind one million times stronger.

Our conscious and subconscious minds work together. The conscious mind focuses on control: the subconscious mind takes the wheel when we are unfocused. Cognitive neuroscientists say we are conscious of about five percent of our cognitive activity when we are highly focused. Therefore, 95 percent of the time, we create our reality from our subconscious mind. It's the reason change and recovery are so massively challenging.

∞

Two Minds

Despite our conscious mind telling us that "we are enough," the subconscious tells us we're not. No matter what others say, "I am not enough" will remain our true belief unless we do the critical work of reprogramming our subconscious mind.

Dad's way to parent was to criticize and sometimes humiliate me. I am sure he had good intentions and thought it would make me want to do better. It did the opposite. It created a false belief that I lacked worth. Negative self-perceptions become wired in our brain and embedded in our cells, building the foundation of our mistaken identity.

It's no wonder I'd overreact to anyone criticizing me. However, after my years of acceptance, reprogramming, and awakening, thoughts of inferiority don't affect me as they once did. Through self-awareness, I can now recognize the old lies quickly and even laugh at the old voices, knowing it's only my past programming, not who I am.

It took a ton of work to get to this peaceful place to observe the "I-am-not-enough" voice without reacting.

I had to bravely face "I am not enough" by re-experiencing the emotions of wanting my father to affirm that I was worthy as a little boy because I carried this pain-body right into adulthood.

I began embracing and being kind to myself. After all, it was my own past belief, not that of someone else or my father. Playing the victim was of no use. I learned how to hold the "I am not enough" part of me and not be ashamed. The message was not going to drive my bus anymore.

Remember, we will continue to recreate negative experiences despite our commitment not to revisit them. Enslaved to the subconscious mind that will go to any length to protect itself, we will continue to sabotage ourselves.

∞

Early Development

The early development of the subconscious mind is contingent on our environment and the genetics of our family tree's strengths and weaknesses. Proper development is stunted through abuse and emotional loss, stressful environments, addicted or unstable parents or caretakers, fear-based

"In our first seven years of life, we learn by hypnosis, which means all data is downloaded straight into the subconscious mind; we bypass the conscious mind. Next, we learn by repetition; we repeat repeatedly, and it becomes our hard-wired programming. It's known as habitual/ repetition learning, and it's how we learn our ABCs and math."
~ *Dr. Bruce Lipton, cell biologist, author, an international leader in epigenetics*

religious programming, and other experiences.

∞

A New Program for a New Life

Reprogramming the subconscious mind requires establishing new neural pathways through repetition. Just as consistent workouts build muscle, a consistent recovery program is necessary for awakening and long-term recovery.

A few ways to reprogram the subconscious mind:

Daily meditation is one of the most effective ways to reprogram the subconscious mind. When we meditate regularly, our focus on the present moment helps us see how our subconscious programming impacts our thoughts and emotions. The subconscious is most receptive to reprogramming in morning and night-time meditation, prayers, and gratitude.

Affirmative Prayer, such as the one below, are another way to help break the stranglehold of limiting beliefs.

Example: "I let go of all the things that no longer serve me. As I let go, I am healed and made whole. My life is blessed, and I am grateful for all that I have."

You can find other affirmative prayers at the end of the book.

Yoga includes many different traditions and paths. Today there is even yoga for twelve-step recovery.

Events such as the birth or death of a loved one or a near-death experience sometimes pierce the subconscious mind and reveal an opportunity for a massive shift in consciousness. The surgery experience I described at the beginning of this book is an example of this type of event.

Energy Psychology uses noninvasive methods to access the subconscious mind to heal trauma and self-limiting, self-sabotaging beliefs. Some of these modalities include *Emotional Freedom Technique* (EFT) that employs "tapping" to work directly with body energy; *Eye Movement Desensitization and Reprocessing* (EMDR), an interactive psychotherapy technique; and *PSYCH-K (psychological kinesiology)*, a method that uses kinesiology and other healing systems.

Compassionate Inquiry is a psychotherapeutic approach developed by Dr. Gabor Maté. Through Compassionate Inquiry, the client can recognize the unconscious dynamics that run their lives and how to liberate themselves from them.

I went through the Intensive One-Year Compassion Inquiry course with Gabor and now use it with my clients.

Ayahuasca Ceremonies have been used as a healing medicine by the Amazonians for thousands of years. Many studies on Ayahuasca show it is beneficial in treating anxiety, depression, trauma, and addictions. This sacred medicine is composed of two main ingredients: the leaves of the Psychotria Viridis plant and the stalks of the Banisteriopsis Caapi vine. Together, they produce a remarkable and potentially life-altering hallucinogenic medicine that goes to the heart of our subconscious mind. It's also known as the mother of rebirth.

> "The purpose of Compassionate Inquiry is to drill down to the core stories people tell themselves—to get them to see what story they are telling themselves unconsciously; what those beliefs are, where they came from; and guide them to the possibility of letting go of those stories, or letting go of the hold those stories have on them ... That's what Compassionate Inquiry is."
> ~ Dr. Gabor Maté

In 2017, after considerable investigation, I decided to try Mother Ayahuasca to evolve my consciousness further and heal some old subconscious patterns. The plant substance was administered and monitored by a shaman Maestro, and I will never forget my experience; it was profound. I tell others interested in Ayahuasca to do their investigation, meditation, and prayer to see if it calls them as it did me.

In Alcoholic Anonymous official biography, *Pass It On*, a whole chapter was devoted to founder Bill Wilson's medically supervised experimentation with LSD in 1956.

On page 371: "Bill was enthusiastic about his experience with LSD; he felt it helped him eliminate barriers erected by the self, or ego, that stand in the way of one's direct experience of the cosmos and God. He thought he might have found something that could make a big difference to the lives of many who still suffered."[13]

It caused considerable controversy within AA, and Bill stopped participating.

Quick note: I do not believe in one way to heal or reprogram the subconscious because the spiritually awakened life is an inner journey, never a destination.

∞

Nonbelief

Living life in the present moment, through unfiltered lenses without the influence of past conditioning, allows us to freely ask questions about our current belief system and be open to the answers.

All the major religions maintain universal truths like "to receive love, we must give it away" and "treat others as you would like to be treated." These are truths I call true knowledge. But, if we believe our religion is the only truth, we are using it in our ego's service.

> "We are really alive only when we live in nonbelief—open, waiting, trusting, and loving to do what appears in front of us now." [14]
> ~Byron Katie, self-inquiry speaker and author

∞

A Declaration of Commitment to Truth, Love, and Peace

"I will support beliefs that empower and let go of those that don't. I will practice the power of nonbelief by living fully in the present moment."

LAYER EIGHT

PERSONALITY

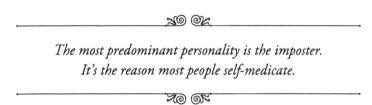

The most predominant personality is the imposter.
It's the reason most people self-medicate.

Personality is a combination of thoughts, feelings, and behaviors that makes us unique in the physical world. It's how we express ourselves and how others see us.

For decades, most psychologists believed personality to be unchanging. However, a new fifty-year study[15] confirmed what the great spiritual teachers have been saying for eons—that personality is both stable and changing from birth onward.

Personality traits, behaviors, and beliefs helped me make sense of my childhood, but others became a liability as I grew older. Just as rusted tools no longer work properly, the tools we've used to survive may block us from developing loving relationships and knowing our authentic self. A fearless search and compassionate peeling away of the layers of our mistaken identity, not willpower, is the way to let go of unhelpful or undesirable personality traits.

∞

Addiction and Being a Highly Sensitive Person

Anyone who has ever watched puppies playing knows that each was born with an original personality. It's no different for humans. We do not understand what influences or factors are responsible for our unique personality at birth, but we must trust and have faith that there are good reasons and a purpose for it.

I was definitely born an HSP (highly sensitive person) compared to my brother and sister. My mom would confirm. We HSPs tend to experience emotional pain more strongly than others, making us more susceptible to addiction, depression, and other issues.

As a child, I was mercilessly criticized, teased, and put down for being a highly sensitive person (HSP). I saw my sensitivity as a weakness and denied it.

The truth is that the most robust and creative people—artists, writers, visionaries, creators, musicians, and healers—are HSPs. Many of us in recovery are not only highly sensitive but extremely creative.

I would argue that most of us cannot move beyond addiction without a deeper understanding and acceptance of our sensitive nature. I had to face my own by being vulnerable with other compassionate people, or I would have continued use my substance of choice. Accepting my highly sensitive nature helped me let go of the shame I carried. Today, I see my highly sensitive personality as a priceless gift, not the curse I thought it was.

Dr. Elaine Aron offers families an opportunity to understand and honor the traits of children in *The Highly Sensitive Person: How To Thrive When the World Overwhelms You,* "In one family, a quiet artist who does not like sports will be considered ideal. In another, this child will be a huge disappointment. But there is always a good fit when parents accept their children for who they are, then adapt their methods to suit the child."

I had to stop trying to fit in and be true to myself by not caring when others criticized and teased me for my sensitivity. As it's said, What others say about us is not of our business.

∞

The Ego

The ego has been around as a biological survival mechanism since we first climbed out of the trees. The ego is not a big mistake but a limitation of our true nature.

Believing the ego is only negative often leads people to create a shame-based, puffed-up version of themselves to cover their insecurities. But remember the ego can also play the other side of the street with "poor me."

If we want less ego, we must wake up more to our true nature. Self-awareness is the path. Following it often helps me keep my ego in check.

> "Love says, 'I am everything.' Wisdom says, 'I am nothing.' Between the two, my life flows."
> ~Nisargadatta Maharaj, Hindu guru of nondualism

∞

A Declaration of Commitment to Truth, Love, and Peace

"I choose to embrace and celebrate my unique personality. I can share all of myself whenever I choose."

LAYER NINE

THE BODY

We are deathless, eternal beings, not our bodies.

Body awareness begins in kids as young as four to six months old. The obsession that love, acceptance, and success depend on a particular look follows.

My flaming red hair, many freckles, big ears, and heightened sensitivity as a little boy made me the target of teasing from other kids and reinforced for me a message that my appearance was unacceptable.

My dad was a TV sportscaster, an incredible athlete who competed in many sports, and always on a diet. He teased me about being fat and made judgmental comments about overweight women under the guise of kidding around. I even remember him telling mom in a humorous way that he would divorce her if she became obese and I am sure it affected my baby sister the most.

I became a fitness freak to protect myself from men and to attract success, the perfect woman, and friends. The media and society continued to reinforce my false belief that I was my body, promoting an obsession with physical appearance, abilities, and attributes that affect most western societies and boost the myths and phobias of aging and death.

My focus on my physical body grew to epic proportions when I discovered weight lifting. Yet, despite winning the 1990 Mr.

Ottawa Overall Bodybuilding Championship, the next morning, I was barely able to look at myself in the mirror. My mistaken identity told me I was still fat and ugly.

I suffered for years before I understood that having a pumped-up body had nothing to do with being worthy of love or happiness. Nothing! The body is our vessel we honor and look after, but in no way does it have anything to do with who we are. I still love hitting the gym, but now, I feel comfortable in my skin.

Had Dad not taught me the importance of health and fitness, I might be dead. My heart would never have survived the massive hits from years of addiction. For Dad's influence on health and fitness, I am grateful. My seventy-eight-year-old father only recently stopped teaching skiing in the Rocky Mountains, and he continues to work out regularly. You go, Dad!

∞

Love Transcends the Body

Nicole and I had been together for four years. She was the woman I wanted to marry and have children with, but we had recently broken up because of my addiction. Believing it would be a temporary separation, I returned to Toronto in 1997 while she taught grades four and five in Saskatoon. I'd put together a few months of clean time and was working a decent recovery program, so I was ready to have Nicole back in my life. We planned to talk after she returned from an out-of-town weekend. While she was gone, I had the most intense and vivid dream of my life. The highway was dark and glistening as the rain bounced off the pavement. Nicole was driving her old Mustang down the S-shaped road, and, as usual, we were laughing. The slippery road made the car feel unstable. I shouted at her to slow down for the tight left turn. Prepared for the vehicle to roll, I held her with both arms to protect her from the coming crash.

The intensity of the dream made it seem so real! I woke up and couldn't go back to sleep. After I dressed, I walked into the living room and wrote in my diary, "I pray for you today, Nicole! I pray for YOU!"

A few hours later, I returned from a bistro to hear the phone ringing. My friend Vanessa was calling to tell me that Nicole tried to pass a transport truck and lost control on loose gravel, rolled her car, and died the night before at University Hospital.

This crisis was different from the ongoing ones of my life. I lost my breath, then caught myself from hitting the floor.

Over 500 people attended her funeral, but I wasn't one of them. I went on a death run to numb the pain of believing in a sick, twisted way that her death was my fault, wondering if she had never met me, would she still be alive. It's amazing what shock and grief will do to one's mind.

The next five years of using and wanting to die were all I knew. I went to treatment in those dark days and even planted a tree in Nicole's name at Stonehenge Treatment Centre, relapsing immediately after leaving treatment.

At Cedar Lodge my grieving finally began. Dwayne Cameron, a counselor and now a good friend, drove me to her grave, where I broke down, made my peace, and felt her loving arms wrap around me. It's a day I will never forget.

Four more years would pass before I could acknowledge and accept that Nicole had sent me her loving energy at the minute of her death through that dream. It gave me a sweet testimony of our connection, one of eternally awakened consciousness that death would never sever.

It is with great reverence for Nicole's life, and not with paralyzing sadness and a life-threatening addiction, that I celebrate her today. I'm sure she is smiling because I am awake and in long-term recovery, and because she loved to teach, and this was her teaching moment. In your loving memory, Nicole, thank you for reminding me to celebrate life and know that I am an eternal spiritual being, not a body.

∞

Science and the Body

Science views the human body through many lenses:

- The human body is made of a long list of chemical ingredients. Oxygen is the most abundant (65% by mass), followed by carbon (18%), hydrogen (10%), nitrogen (3%), calcium (1.4%), and phosphorus (1.1%).[16]
- Between 30 to 40 trillion cells, over 200 different kinds, each with different weight and size, are in the body.
- The space in and between each atom is far greater than the atom itself. In other words, the human body is 99.99999 percent space, no different from all the matter in the universe.

Scientists now believe that all matter consists of microscopic vibrating strings of energy, that the physical world we see consists of electromagnetic waves of light. According to the Law of Conservation of Energy, energy can neither be created nor destroyed. It can only be transformed or transferred from one form to another. Energy is eternal, meaning our physical body is 100 percent eternal energy. I believe that when the body dies, our endless, boundless energy shifts into a new form. Understanding that we are energy means we are all deathless.[17]

I found it difficult to let go of the false belief that I was my body. Yet my faith in both science

> "Science without religion is lame; religion without science is blind."
> ~Albert Einstein, physicist

and spirituality continues to point me in the direction of an ever-evolving awakened consciousness.

∞

A Declaration of Commitment to Truth, Love, and Peace

"My body is not who I am. The real me is beyond the limits of a body. I release any negative body images. I honor my body as a vessel for my spirit."

LAYER TEN

FEAR

*F.E.A.R: False Evidence Appearing Real
or Face Everything and Recover.*

Fear is one of the biggest blocks to our recovery; the more we try to escape or avoid it, the worse our fear becomes. Fear needs to be bravely faced by shining light upon it. Only then can Love intervene.

People in active addiction or early recovery live in a fear-based reality, feeding it with doubts that they are not good enough, unworthy of love, likely to get hurt, or won't find lasting recovery. Making things more difficult is the stigma of addiction flaming the fears of rejection.

I used denial, dishonesty, manipulation, and acting out as strategies to survive and calm my ongoing physical, emotional and spiritual

> "The cave you fear to enter holds the treasure you seek."
> ~Joseph Campbell,
> author, editor, professor

anxiety. I carried these coping strategies right into adulthood, and they grew more with each relapse. They are what the twelve-step world calls *character defects*. These defects were the strategies we used as children to protect ourselves. I now call them *character issues*. Calling them *defects* adds more rocks to the backpack of shame.

I wrote an inventory of how fear ruled my life, then shared my findings with someone I trusted. An important step, but I had to go deeper to find my freedom from fear.

∞

Ten Discoveries That Changed My Relationship with Fear

1. Fear hijacks the mind in such a way that we believe we are in danger. Or, we carry forward some unhealed past events that we think might happen again. In other words, fear is never about now. Fear is thoughts about some future time that does not exist, which causes us to suffer unnecessarily.

2. Thanks to evolution, we have a brain that once alerted us to take action when in danger. Despite today's rarity of hungry saber-toothed tigers, our brain continued to evolve and use fear as a call for action against any real or perceived threats. Understanding that fear is normal helped me to not judge myself harshly when I felt afraid. We reduce the power of fear when we recognize it.

3. We aren't afraid of the unknown. We are fearful of the known coming to an end. For example, *we* are not scared of death; we fear losing the people, places, ideas, and experiences we call our lives.

   The Latin phrase, *memento mori* (Remember, you must die), is designed to inspire, motivate, and clarify death as something to embrace. Working through our denial of death sets us free from anxiety, fear, and undue suffering.

74

> "Nothing is more creative than death since it has the whole secret of life. It means that the past must be abandoned, that the unknown cannot be avoided, that 'I' cannot continue, and that nothing can be ultimately fixed. When a man knows this, he lives for the first time in his life. By holding his breath, he loses it. By letting go, he finds it."
>
> ~Alan Watts, author, speaker

4. Many fears spring from the ego. It asks, "Will I fit in or be snubbed? Do they like me or dislike me?" When fear enters our relationships, issues like dishonesty and manipulation come into play. A self-centered person is a fear-based person.

5. Fear is pain in disguise. When we attach our identity to external things like a new car or a high-paying job, we may fear losing them.

6. Fear is based entirely upon beliefs that are, at best, incomplete and some are false. I continue to work with many clients who are

> "The constant assertion of belief is an indication of fear."
> ~Jiddu Krishnamurti, philosopher, writer, speaker

still trying to undo the horror of their religious upbringing.

7. Fear is a state of unconsciously forgetting who we are. All healing is a release from fear. We are not fear—we are the love beyond it.

8. The presence of fear is a sure sign that we are trusting in our strength (ego) and have forgotten about being One with Love. Faith

> "A miracle is just a shift in perception from fear to love."
> ~Marianne Williamson, author, spiritual leader, politician, activist

is remembering the One Power and letting its strength take the place of our weakness. The instant we are willing to do this, there is indeed nothing to fear. We "let go and let God."

9. Fear cautions us not to put our hand on a hot stove, jump off a balcony, or cheat on our partner. But what if intelligence was all that was required to keep us safe? Fear might provide some short-term motivation. For example, the fear of relapse can move us to take action, but it can also create unnecessary stress. Fear is the ego trying to protect us, but it never works in the long run.

10. When we face our fears, especially during our most challenging times, we have the

> Fear kills more dreams than failure.

opportunity to make our most significant victories. Everything we have ever wanted, needed, or dreamed of is on the other side of fear.

Worry Is Another Word for Fear

Imagine a majestic, 300-year-old red oak tree deep in the forest. Over the years, it has been hit by lighting countless times, nearly destroyed in a forest fire, survived a few avalanches, hurricanes, floods, and other traumatic events. But unseen are small, seemingly inconsequential bugs, slowly and steadily eating away at its base that will ultimately destroy the tree.

How many of us are like this tree? We're able to survive traumatic events, but an accumulation of small issues (the bugs), poorly managed, takes us down. These little bugs are life's worries (fear). They can slowly kill us if we allow them.

Robert L. Leahy's *The Worry Cure: Seven Steps to Stop Worry from Stopping You* includes the results of a study in which subjects had to write down their worries over an extended period, then later identify which did and did not happen. It turned out that 85 percent the subjects' worries didn't occur. Of the 15 percent of the worries that occurred, the subjects reported that they handled the difficulty better than expected or that the struggle taught them a valuable lesson. This study shows that the lion's share of worries is only our fearful mind punishing us with exaggeration and misperception. When I choose to focus on my fears and try to exert control over the universe, things seldom go well.

The more awake I become, the more value I see in trusting the universe. I take on whatever the universe gives me by putting one

> "There isn't enough room in your life for both worry and faith. You must decide which one will live there."
> ~Reverend Lorraine Trout

foot in front of the other. I keep my primary purpose in the Now, and everything generally works out in the end.

What fear requires is our attention and compassion so it can go back to the nothingness from which it came.

> Find out more about how Everything We Want Is on the Other Side of F.E.A.R., False Evidence Appearing Real.
> https://youtu.be/zqhBMAbFEvQ

Remember, what we resist will persist.

∞

A Declaration of Commitment to Truth, Love, and Peace

"It's okay to have fears, but I am not my fears. When I feel afraid, I open my heart, seek the truth, and courageously choose to let Love and faith dissolve my fear."

SECTION C

THE SEVEN HEALING PRINCIPLES OF AWAKENING

Peeling the layers of our mistaken identity can be challenging. The following seven healing principles are the essential tools to help us wake up.

HEALING PRINCIPLE 1

KNOWING WE ARE LOVE

꘎ ✿ ✿

When we give and receive love, we experience the divine.

✿ ✿

Love is a way of describing absolute reality, the energy that underpins everything in the universe. God, Source, Higher Power, Higher Self, and my favorite, The Nameless, are just a few names people call the energy of Love. This Love energy is the essence of *being* inside all of us.

Love is the glue that holds us and everything else together, a unified field that seems hidden. Just as fish swimming in the ocean may be unaware of the water, many of us swim in a sea of Love, utterly oblivious of its presence.

> "Love is a state of Being. Your Love is not outside; it is deep within you. You can never lose it, and it cannot leave you."
>
> ~Eckhart Tolle, spiritual leader, author

Using drugs numbed the false belief that I was unlovable and gave me a fabricated sense of love. It was no wonder I became programmed to believe love was something outside myself.

> "You can only accept the level of love outside of you at the level you accept it within yourself."
>
> ~Kyle Cease, author, comedian, spiritual teacher

I spent much of my life pursuing love from others

in various ways that never worked, and I ended up feeling even more rejected and addicted.

At its core, addiction is the shutting down of the heart chakra. When that happens, we lose ourselves, then develop ways to cope with our loss. Some become abusers (hurt people, hurt others), others play the victim card or develop codependency, others acquire bigger-than-life egos or other disorders and dysfunctions.

They say the longest journey is the one from the mind to the heart. I say absolutely, especially when it comes to recovery. My spiritual awakening began when my mind and heart connected after many years of hard work.

The idea that "you just need to love yourself more" is expressed in countless self-help books, articles, and blogs. I am sure you have said it to yourself over and over without any

> "Everyone has love, but it can only come out when he/she is convinced of the impossibility and the frustration of trying to love himself/herself."
> –Alan Watts, author, speaker

success. The truth is we can't just consciously decide one day to love ourselves and–bam–we love ourselves. We have to take action because love is a verb. Dig a little deeper, and you'll see the fundamental flaw within "*I* just need to love *myself* more." As there cannot be two of you, one does not exist. I was blocked from knowing Love as my true nature because I was trying to convince the ego-self, that doesn't exist, to love myself. Instead of taking recovery action for the real me, I was wasting my time.

When we try to love ourselves, we fight our minds' illusions. The essence of awakening is the continual letting go of the idea of a separate self (ego) instead, letting the One Love run the show. Spiritual gurus, sages, yoga masters, and other awakened people through the ages have understood that no being or event happens in isolation. All things and all beings are connected. Zen master and spiritual leader Thich Nhat Hanh calls this "interbeing."

That separation is an illusion is one of the greatest spiritual truths, one that's hard to comprehend. With so much conflict and division in the world, humanity needs this truth more than ever.

> "The greatest illusion of this world is the illusion of separation. Things you think are separate and different are actually one and the same."
>
> ~Guru Pathik, avatar guru

Now, think of Oneness as a gigantic rubber ball that has always existed. Outside the ball is darkness. Inside is pure light. A tiny pinhole in the ball shines a bright ray of light (Consciousness) into an expression of life. One pinhole delivers a human being; another delivers an animal, another a tree, and so on. There are now countless rays of the One Light, each delivering Life expressions from the same Source.

When our single pinhole begins to close, we experience death in this world. However, our ray of light remains inside the ball. We are deathless, eternal beings of light. We are back to our Source; we are home. There is no separate me or you. There is only One Light, One Life that only appears to be separate. The spiritual truth of Oneness in your heart lets you know that you only hurt yourself if you hurt someone else.

When we awaken, we feel, witness, and know It is everywhere. Love in human relationships—the connection—is an expression of a larger, all-encompassing, universal love.

∞

Spiritual Pride

It is easy to cross the line of spirituality and lose our humility in the pursuit of enlightenment. Even spirituality can become dogmatic through people's pride. Spiritual pride may tell us that our spiritual practice is not good enough, that we must be more positive and in the *now*, or that we must be doing something wrong if we're not feeling well. It may also give us the false belief that our spiritual practice is better than that of others, or even worse—that we are more spiritual than others, yet another false identity.

Thinking there is a magical formula to spiritual awakening is a bullshit story. Don't follow anyone claiming to have the best and only way. Spiritual perfectionism is about trying to impress others in a game of one-upmanship, unaware that the ego-mind has taken over. When we practice spiritual pride or perfectionism, our underlying belief is that we are failing.

Spiritual pride happens the most when we do not practice unconditional self-acceptance by treating our human side with just as much respect, honor, and love as our divinity.

Remember, we came here to be messy and beautiful. We must not deny our humanness and must understand spiritual awakening is not linear—it's up and down, sideways, and all around, and sometimes there is even a long desert period. By knowing this, we can use all of it for the expansion of our consciousness.

We are all 100 percent spiritual beings! No one is better than anyone else. The only difference between any two persons: one might be more aware of their 100 percent spiritual beingness at that current moment than the other. Having this awareness helps me stay humble and not judge the recovery or spiritual practices of others.

Zen teaches us to stay in the center of *Yin* and *Yang*; both are vital. Balance is the key, and effortless effort the way.

∞

A Declaration of Commitment to Truth, Love, and Peace

"I acknowledge that Love is my birthright. I am a manifestation of Love."

HEALING PRINCIPLE 2

CONNECTION

.ᴔ© ©ᴣ.

Disconnection with others is the death of recovery.

ᴔ© ©ᴣ

In the 1960s, addiction research scientists conducted a study where they isolated rats in separate cages. Each rat had a lever in its cage to push to access drugs. In response, the rats consumed drugs until they overdosed and died. The scientists concluded that the drugs the rats consumed were irresistibly addictive.

Dr. Bruce K. Alexander and his team at Simon Fraser University saw the study differently. Since rats are highly social, sexual, and industrious, were the drugs merely a way to escape their loneliness and isolation? He and his colleagues built a colossal plywood box on the laboratory floor with platforms for climbing, tin cans for hiding, wood, and running wheels for exercise, then filled it with lots of rats of both sexes. The rats loved Rat Park.[18]

They ran two separate experiments comparing rats' drug consumption in Rat Park with those confined alone in laboratory cages. In virtually every trial, the rats in solitary confinement consumed more drugs, and many died. Meanwhile, Rat Park rats had little interest in drugs and thrived, as did the resulting crowd of baby rats.

Dr. Alexander's study revealed that the rats were drawn to drugs only to respond to their isolated environment and lack of connection.

From this and other research, Johann Hari coined, *"The opposite of addiction is not sobriety. It is human connection."*

His statement echoes a belief many addiction experts have espoused for years, that addiction is about numbing the pain from our inability to connect in healthy ways. Just as in Rat Park, addiction isolates people in cages built with the bars of trauma, toxic shame, false beliefs, stress, and fear.

∞

Trauma: The Strongest Bar in Our Cage

Trauma slowly kills our spirit because we miss out on acquiring an essential sense of connection and safety to our environment.

Most people do not want to accept that their unhealed childhood experiences created a template of suffering and pain in their adult lives. We learn the good, bad, and ugly from our caregivers and childhood environment. Telling ourselves later to "get over it" or "I had a normal childhood" are both forms of denial

> "Children are, by definition, dependent, and their dependency means that the nature of their family relationships profoundly influences their experiences in both health and illness. Attachment can be understood as being the enduring emotional closeness which binds families in order to prepare children for independence and parenthood."[19]
> - Corinne Rees, researcher, author

that will affect not only our lives but every relationship and those of future generations.

∞

My Cage

I felt alone, lost, different, and disconnected, even when I was around my friends and family. My bigger-than-life personality hid my feelings. As a teen and young adult, I had high social skills, lots of good-time buddies, and was the life of the party. I was a masterful actor who never left the stage because I feared the real me was not good enough. The mistaken identity that I carried in adulthood was an attempt to protect myself from possible harm.

I turned to substances because I felt alone, then I felt alone because I couldn't stop using. I called my dilemma the revolving door of loneliness.

Self-abandonment and self-rejection constantly played in my life because I craved intimate, safe, dependable, empathetic, and loving relationships. But unconsciously, I let no one in because of my fear of being hurt. This fear led to attention-seeking that only pushed people away, leaving me feeling more lonely.

> "At the innermost core of all loneliness is a deep and powerful yearning for union with one's lost self."
> ~Brendan Behan, poet, short story writer, novelist, playwright

When I found cocaine, I felt a sense of connection, albeit a false one, for the first time in my life.

∞

Part of My Healing

My psychologist, Nayyar Javed, who had extensive experience working with childhood trauma and Eastern spiritual practices, helped me discover and heal from what I experienced as a child. I am grateful that I sought outside help beyond twelve-step recovery. Her spiritual guidance and psychological help are equally responsible for the joy in my today.

∞

Disconnection

My mistaken identity and descent into addiction harmed the relationships I had with my family. My mom and sister Lana describe their lives during my pattern of relapse and recovery as living life on a roller coaster.

Mom says she was scared to answer the phone, afraid it might be someone trying to find me, or me begging for money so I wouldn't get killed, or someone calling to tell her I was dead. Her fear lessened a little when I was in jail because she had the comfort of knowing I had a roof over my head and food in my belly. Mom lied to others about my whereabouts, uncertain if it was to protect herself or me. She regrets how her constant concern about me made her neglect my brother, sister, and dad. The level of stress made her feel as if she was losing her marbles. She wanted to help me but didn't know how to do it.

Eventually, she received help for her codependency at the Saint John Addiction and Rehab Centre.

After I called Dad to let him know that I had a cocaine addiction, contemplated suicide, and needed help, he cut off all communication with me. From that day forward, whenever Dad answered the phone, he would say, "Here's your mom," and pass the phone to her. This routine went on for 15 years. He didn't respond to the two closure letters I wrote to him with my counselors' help while in treatment. It hurt me deeply.

I worked with many male clients who shared they too wanted their fathers to say they loved them. I let them know they were not alone and described how I had come to a place of acceptance and forgiveness with Art, my father.

It's heartbreaking that only a few of my male friends in recovery said they had a healthy relationship with their fathers. The rest have no relationship, a damaged one, or fathers who died before they could make peace. We have to stop passing dysfunctions down the line from father to son.

∞

2017

As the family group facilitator at Aurora Treatment Center, I would share the importance of the father and child relationships with the residents' family members and friends. I would encourage the fathers to verbalize their love for their sons and explain how it would help them recover. I remember a male client asking me, "What did you say to my father in the family group? Before he left, he hugged me and whispered that he loved me." With tears in his eyes, he said, "I can't remember the last time Dad said that to me."

The same-sex parent-child relationship is the most important in a child's formative years. If this book helps reunite just one father and son or mother and daughter, it will be well worth it.

> You can change your relationship with your child with a hug and saying I love you.

∞

Codependent Relationships

A person with codependency believes their well-being depends on controlling and changing another person's behavior. Attaching their identity to others, they lose control of their own ability to think, feel, act, and take care of themselves. They are addicted to the other person. Until they realize their recovery lies not in the other person (no matter how much they believe it does) but in themselves, they will never change.

Another part of codependency is the people pleasing and enabling. The codependency person actual believes they are being selfless but in reality, the enabling is all about them and their inability to confront their feelings of guilt or shame or inferiority.

The roots of codependency are usually formed by childhood traumatic experiences of an alcoholic or abusive parent or another authority figure. Sometimes the origins of codependency are from later in life, perhaps from an abusive adult relationship as one example.

Detaching from the person of our obsession is the first step in recovery. Only they can work on themselves and connect to Source (God). The *Bhagavad Gita,* a work central to Hinduism, says, "Detachment is not that we own nothing, but that nothing should own us."

Another word for detachment and one that I prefer is non-attachment. Non-attachment means we are all responsible only for ourselves. It's not our job to fix, solve, or worry about problems that are not our own. It's about loving those we care about without enabling them by setting and keeping boundaries with ourselves and them. Self-love and self-respect come to us when we take care of ourselves.

> "When we can't stop thinking, talking about or worrying about someone or something; when our emotions are churning and boiling; when we feel like we have to do something about someone because we can't stand it another minute; when we're hanging on by a thread, and it feels like that single thread is frayed; and when we believe we can no longer live with the problem we've been trying to live with. It's time to detach! You will learn to recognize when detachment is advisable. A good rule of thumb is: You need to detach most when it seems the least likely or possible thing to do."[20]
>
> ~Melody Beattie, self-help, addiction and recovery author

As they say in the recovery rooms, "Put down the magnifying glass and pick up the mirror." Our

Learn more in my video, Can You Say No?
https://youtu.be/Zq1inmXCvXE

efforts to control or cling only create anxiety. To enjoy life and its pleasures, we must let go, and let it *be*.

∞

Healthy Connections

Mentor/Sponsor. I have been fortunate to have benefited from the wisdom, strength, and compassion from great mentors, especially Reverend Lorraine and Reverend Darrell Gudmundson. Darrell passed on July 1, 2013 from cancer. I would not be the person I am today without them. I will never forget Reverend Lorraine telling me when we met twenty-six years ago, "I'm here to help you remember Love is who you are until you can fully believe it for yourself."

Friends in Recovery. The open, vulnerable, and compassionate relationships in the recovery rooms are among the most important in my life. With love and support from my recovery friends, I slowly began to trust again.

∞

Romance in Recovery

In January 2017, I hadn't been in a long-term committed relationship for over eighteen years. I had a few one- or three-month relationships, but nothing more. I was OK with that because I enjoyed my own company. However, a part of me wanted a spiritual life partner. Those "wanting feelings" drove me a little crazy, so I chatted with my good friend and family therapist Cheryl Cohan who worked at the same treatment center with me on beautiful Lake Winnipeg. After I asked why I was bothered by feelings of wanting to have an intimate relationship, she opened my eyes.

"Even though you are in long-term recovery, Paul, the pull of wanting a relationship goes much deeper than belonging for you because you had to overcome an addiction. The "wanting feelings" for a relationship are triggering your memories of wanting your substance of choice and the powerlessness you felt over it. In other words, wanting a loving relationship and overcoming your addiction makes your feelings that much more emotional. It is no wonder that you do not like the feeling of *wanting* someone or *wanting* anything for that matter.

"Our need to belong goes beyond the need for superficial social ties or sexual interactions; it is a need for meaningful, profound bonding. A sense of belongingness is crucial to our well-being. The bottom line is that we are all naturally driven toward establishing and sustaining belongingness."

Whether you're new or in long-term recovery, please understand that wanting to have a loving relationship is a healthy human desire. I recommend that those in the first year of recovery build a relationship with themselves. Sexual, romantic relationships during this time often result in relapse.

∞

Relationships Are Mirrors

All relationships are holy encounters that show us everything that holds us back from knowing the Love within ourselves and others. The primary purpose of relationships is to challenge ourselves to grow without fixing the other person.

> When we judge others, we judge ourselves.
> How we treat others is how we treat ourselves.
> What we give out, we get back.
> The qualities we admire in others are also within ourselves.
> The qualities we dislike in others are also within ourselves or
> once were.
> When I fully accept you, I fully accept me.
> When I unconditionally love you, I unconditionally love myself.
> When I forgive you, I forgive myself.
> When I bless you, I bless myself.

I see soulmate relationships as two rough rocks, each polishing the other's rough edges to create two beautiful stones [souls].

∞

Consider a Pet

In 2015, I made living amends to Tiny when, after a long search, I found Sharona at a small dog rescue. She is family, and no amount of money could ever convince me to give her away. Sharona helped me pull out the final daggers of unhealed trauma that were still piercing my heart. Her unconditional love propelled my spirit to love her back unselfishly.

All dogs are sentient beings of pure and divine free-spirited energy. Their direct connection to spirit, unconditional love, and acceptance speeds our healing in ways beyond understanding. Our pets share love, joy, humor, and peace with us without saying a word. Those who teach us the most about humanity aren't always human.

It is recommended not to take responsibility for a pet until your second substance-free year. Care for a plant for your first year. If it lives, you may be ready for a pet!

∞

Spend Time in Nature

I once meditated at the base of the famous Chateau Lake Louise while on vacation, followed by self-inquiry, the practice of asking a bold question to higher consciousness and listening for an answer.

Question: Why do I need to spend time in nature?

Answer: Have you ever told an ocean it was ugly, Paul? The Rocky Mountains, they're not good enough? The moon, it didn't belong? Criticized the Milky Way or the way birds fly? Probably never!

Then, why do we accept, love, and cherish nature and do the opposite to ourselves and others? The entire human race is part of nature, not separate from it. Nature speaks to our heart, not the mind of judgment. Spend more time in nature, and you will treat yourself and all others with more reverence.

Exposure to nature not only makes us feel better emotionally but contributes to our physical well-being as it reduces our blood pressure, slows our heart rate, releases muscle tension, and lowers stress hormone production.

Everyone is interconnected and has an essential role in the whole of nature. None of us are different from the rest of nature. Stop chasing acceptance outside yourself. Your nature is perfect, whole, and complete, just like that of each mountain, lake, and tree. Our nature is a glorious, precious gift.

> "The most experienced life coach you could ever have is nature. She has millions of years of experience managing the entire planet."
>
> *~Dr. Bruce Lipton, cell biologist, author,*
> *and international leader in epigenetics*

∞

A Declaration of Commitment to Truth, Love, and Peace

"I will not allow my feelings of loneliness and disconnection to get in the way of my recovery. I will reach out and connect with others and nature."

HEALING PRINCIPLE 3

SURRENDER

True surrender is standing up and with profound humility,
saying, I do not want to fight with myself or life anymore.

The Western world culture values the individual and individual achievement above all else. It's no wonder the interconnected concepts of powerlessness and surrender send many people running from the rooms before their recovery can begin. I think the real problem is that most don't understand what the word surrender means in the context of recovery. To start the recovery process, we must surrender our whole lives, not just our substance or behavior, although the latter is a great place to start.

Refusing to surrender is refusing to accept reality. Without surrender, we cannot access our spiritual power, and the seeds of recovery can never bear fruit. Surrender is waving the white flag and admitting that we don't have all the answers. It is the collapse of our ego and a new voice, which finally utters, "I need help." Without humility, we are not teachable, and addiction will keep kicking us in the ass.

Surrender is not something we can will, even if we desire it. It cannot come from our intellect. Our intelligence can be the enemy of surrender because it cannot make sense out of it. Surrender must come from the heart, from the gut, from the full understanding of our dilemma.

And the moment we surrender is the moment we have connected to a Higher Power. It's the real reason a lack of surrender is dangerous to recovery.

∞

My Full Surrender

After waking up once again after a minor relapse, I followed my self-critical pattern and made false promises to myself. However, for the first time, I had no desire to continue my relapse (amazing!) and saw no purpose in self-condemnation. When I called Reverend Lorraine to share what had happened, she reminded me that a relapse did not define or negate all the spiritual/recovery work I had done over the past 20 years. I slipped again three days later, but I didn't beat myself up this time. Another five days passed. I used one last time, but this time all self-condemnation was gone. I knew in my heart that my concept of myself was only an illusion created from trauma and pain. I understood that I was not my addiction. I had the first glimpse of the real me. My heart finally accepted the truth that Love was my essence.

My full surrender was awakening to my true nature, and it happened in its own time, not by hitting rock bottom. It occurred when my mind was exhausted and the ego burned up; then I completely let go. The war with my mistaken identity and the voice of addict-man was over. I didn't just surrender the substances of addiction. I surrendered everything on August 2, 2014. Six months later, I realized my desire to use had lifted. It hasn't returned.

Measuring recovery by clean time doesn't necessarily indicate an awakened or a changed person. I've witnessed people with substantial years of sober time who continue to create havoc in their own lives and the lives of others. If we don't do the work, it's easy to switch addictions, replacing booze with pornography, cocaine, gambling, or other substances or behaviors.

∞

Surrender to Love

When I look back over my life, it's apparent that I wasn't afraid of not being enough; the light within petrified me. I was continually running from the light because it felt too much for my fear-based belief system.

> "Our deepest fear is not that we are inadequate. Our deepest fear is that we are powerful beyond measure. It is our light, not our darkness, that most frightens us."[21]
>
> ~Marianne Williamson, author, spiritual leader, politician, activist

Our real battle is accepting that we are all connected and One with Source, It, Love, Higher Power, God—whatever name you use. When we surrender, we finally stop running and look within ourselves.

> "Whenever you're scared to let go of something, the only reason you're scared is that your mind can measure what you will lose. It can't see what you'll gain."
>
> ~Kyle Cease, author, comedian, spiritual teacher

Our mistaken identity prevents us from investigating our inner light with an open mind and heart. Our mistaken identity would rather accept suffering than risk the unknown inner light.

Remember, Spirit, Higher Power, or whatever name we choose is both inside and outside ourselves. Like Islam, Judaism,

> "We found the Great Reality deep down within us. It was only there that He may be found. It was so with us."
>
> ~Alcoholics Anonymous, fourth edition

and Christianity, even theistic religions believe that every life is imbued with the Divine's spirit.

A Surrender Story

Portia Nelson's *There's a Hole in My Sidewalk: The Romance of Self-Discovery* speaks to the process of acceptance and surrender.

> I walk down the street. There is a deep hole in the sidewalk. I fall in. I am lost … I am hopeless. It isn't my fault. It takes forever to find a way out.

> I walk down the same street. There is a deep hole in the sidewalk. I pretend I don't see it. I fall in again. I can't believe I'm in the same place. But it isn't my fault. It still takes a long time to get out.

> I walk down the same street. There is a deep hole in the sidewalk. I see it is there. I still fall in. It's a habit. My eyes are open. I know where I am. It is my fault. I get out immediately.

> I walk down the same street. There is a deep hole in the sidewalk. I walk around it.

> I walk down another street.

∞

After Surrender, Action

A little boy asks, "How did you become so wise, Grandpa?" Grandpa says, "By making the right decisions." The boy then asks, "How do you make the right decisions?" Grandpa replies, "By making a lot of wrong ones."

Like the grandfather, I made many wrong decisions but never gave up on the crucial decision to keep working on my recovery and awakening. I wrote down my choices for greater clarity and insight; I let go of the need to make the perfect decision and talked to my sponsor, mentor, or trusted friend to help discern the truth, and remembered that I could always make another decision. I came to peace, knowing that my decision would either lead to the results I wanted or an opportunity to learn.

∞

Don't Give Up

Robert Downey Jr.'s conversation on *The Oprah Winfrey Show* resonated deeply with me.

"I believe my suffering was for some higher purpose. It is easy to embrace hopelessness when things seem insurmountable, and yet it is just a matter of time before all the elements come together for things to be all right. I believe it's not that difficult to overcome these seemingly ghastly problems. What is hard is to decide. Most difficult situations will resolve themselves if you are persistent and don't give up entirely, and that is precisely what I did, I didn't give up."

It's easy to do well when things are great, but on the days when everything seems to go wrong—when we're tired, broke, frustrated, hungry, and others have lost faith in us—we must continue to stand; these are the days that we make possible our most significant victories.

We all have our challenges. We may become ill, learn we have only months to live, lose our children, or relapse back into an addiction, BUT we must remain *standing*. The

> I will keep standing through all obstacles. I will reach out to others so that they can stand with me. I will show up no matter what happens in my life because I know life is forever changing.

light within me kept me standing during some horrific times in my life.

Our struggles, sufferings, and "un-comfortabilities" can be the gasoline on the fire of our spiritual growth. Overcoming obstacles and circumstances makes us into amazing people. The good news is we don't have to do it alone anymore.

All people have good in them, and all past suffering has powerful messages to help those who still suffer. I am convinced! Love makes all change possible!

∞

Slow Down

Julia Cameron's *The Artist's Way* introduced me to "morning pages," daily free-writing journaling. After doing this practice for 8 years, I recognized a recurring theme that allowed me to avoid slowing down.

My Theme: "To be happy, I need a wonderful girlfriend, blockbuster career, gorgeous house, large savings account, great body, and years of recovery." It was a grand list. Of course, I was never pleased because I had a false belief that happiness was out there when, in fact, it was an inside job.

I saw how I was using busyness to acquire all the outside things to avoid pain and the inner work of awakening and recovery. It was then I made an important decision. I would decide to walk rather than wildly run through my life. I applied this approach to my spirituality, work, exercise, diet, and relationships—and things slowly became better. Go figure. I found the space to deal with my pain.

Surrendering and slowing down work hand in hand because, without them, chances are, we will end up doing it our way once again. And, as I learned from decades of addiction, my way usually didn't work out well.

If we want to enjoy this precious life over the long haul, we need to slow down. Few things of value come from rushing.

> "Surrender is an expression of trust, a way of saying, 'I am available to what wants to emerge through me. I give my consent to it.' It is a recognition that we are cradled by Existence and are ultimately safe and secure, regardless of what enters our experience."
>
> *- Michael Bernard Beckwith, minister, author,*
> *Agape International Spiritual Centre founder*

∞

A Declaration of Commitment to Truth, Love, and Peace

"I accept all that has happened in my life, the good, the bad, and the ugly.

HEALING PRINCIPLE 4

COMPASSION

꩜

Compassion makes it possible to forgive,
love, and know our truth.

꩜

About six years ago, I serendipitously found the Dalai Lama's teachings on compassion everywhere—TV, websites, magazines. Eventually, he had my full attention. After serious self-reflection, I concluded that self-compassion needed to be a must in my life.

> "Compassion is not religious business, it is human business, it is not luxury, it is essential for our own peace and mental stability, it is essential for human survival."
> - *Dalai Lama, highest spiritual teacher of Tibet, Nobel Peace Price winner*

Many never learned how to develop self-compassion in childhood because they had to disconnect from themselves to endure their painful experiences (trauma).

For as long as I could remember, I'd heard a hypercritical voice and did not understand - I blamed myself as a way to survive and cope growing up. There was a part of me that believed self-criticism would motivate me to be a better person and, in turn, win my father's unconditional love and approval. My self-bullying was the result of childhood wounds and zero self-compassion.

Remember, a child will throw out their authenticity in favor of attachment. It was the main reason I desperately sought compassion and acceptance from others and didn't have it for myself.

Self-condemnation and owning others' harsh judgments damage our spirit and wire our addiction stronger in our subconscious mind. It's why the practice of self-compassion is vital. As uncomfortable and squirm-inducing as the idea made me feel, I knew it was time to become my own best friend. By observing the negative messages I was sending to myself, I let go of my old patterns.

> Learning to practice self-compassion can be a complicated process but worth it.

Today even if I do something that is not healthy for my evolution, I continue to practice self-compassion. But it's essential to understand self-compassion isn't a get-out-of-jail-free card. We acknowledge when we screw up, take in whatever learning we can, and promptly make amends if amends are required. Every human being, without exception, makes mistakes. It's a dangerous trick of the addicted brain to hold ourselves to a higher standard than the rest of humanity.

Compassion is part of our true essence. After all, we are mammals that

> We don't serve ourselves or anyone else by putting ourselves down.

would not have survived as a species if not for the wired need for attachment. Compassion is part of who we are.

∞

Compassion from Others

For people still suffering from active addiction and for those who love them, it's important to remember that addiction is a health issue, not moral or criminal. Meeting addiction with anger only increases pain. Compassion is the key. And while treatment centers offer people a safe place to learn about and begin recovery, real recovery begins after leaving treatment.

If society understood pain and trauma as the primary source of addiction, those suffering from an addiction would receive as much compassion as those with cancer. Neither chose to be sick. Both are fighting for their lives.

> "Only in the presence of compassion will people allow themselves to see the truth."
> ~A.H. Almass, American author, spiritual teacher

Only Reverend Lorraine and Mom would take my calls at the height of my addiction. If it were not for these two beautiful, compassionate, loving souls, I might not have made it. Reverend Lorraine told me, "Paul, I'm here to keep reminding you that Love is who you are. One day, you will believe it for yourself." And it happened. I did the work, stripped away my mistaken identity, and remembered Love.

Ego seeks to serve itself. Soul seeks to serve others.
Ego seeks outward recognition. Soul seeks inner authenticity.
Ego sees life as a competition. Soul sees life as a gift.
Ego seeks to preserve self. Soul seeks to preserve others.
Ego looks outward. Soul looks inward.
Ego feels lack. Soul feels abundance.
Ego is mortal. Soul is eternal.
Ego is drawn to lust. Soul is drawn to love.
Ego seeks wisdom. Soul is wisdom.
Ego enjoys the prize. Soul enjoys the process.
Ego is the cause of pain. Soul is the cause of healing.
Ego rejects God [Spirit]. Soul embraces God [Spirit].
Ego is me. Soul is we.

We must refrain from judging people who are unable to accumulate clean time or use medical harm reduction. Choose to see their light, and offer compassion. We must love people as they are, not as we think they should be.

The etymology of the word compassion stems from the Latin *com* meaning "with, together" and the Latin *pati* "to suffer." It's the feeling that motivates people to help others. It's how we shine our light. All through the ages, spiritual teachers have made compassion a central practice. There are examples of genuine compassion in the thousands of recovery meetings every single day around the world.

All it takes to make a difference is one person reaching out their hand, saying, "I'm here for you. I've been where you are. I care about you. You're not alone." I know I wouldn't have the life I have today if not for the many people in recovery who showed me compassion, who saw the light within me when others could not.

∞

Humility and Compassion

Humility gives us freedom from pride or arrogance, an essential component of compassion. It allows us to accept ourselves and others as equals. It's our mistaken identity that tells us differently. My friend Heather, the director of a treatment center where I worked, said, "I see sugar and shit in everyone."

We can only guess or think we know what another person might feel. Compassion helps us remember that we all have our strengths and challenges. We're all doing the best we can with the resources we have.

∞

Compassion in Action

I lived for a year at Streets to Homes, a somewhat controversial homeless shelter in the heart of the club district in downtown Toronto. The shelter's mission was to give people with addictions and mental illness shelter while helping them find affordable housing. Unlike most shelters, it had no curfew, served excellent food, and was clean. While we couldn't use or drink in the building, what we did outside was our business.

The shelter's goal was not sobriety but to treat everyone in addiction with compassion. If we wanted abstinence, shelter staff would support and help us. The compassion and kindness I received there, even when I relapsed, was epic. They remained kind and supportive until I had enough courage to leave the nest.

∞

A Declaration of Commitment to Truth, Love, and Peace

"Compassion is essential to finding lasting recovery. Every day I will exercise compassion for myself and others through my words, actions, and deeds."

HEALING PRINCIPLE 5

UNCONDITIONAL SELF-ACCEPTANCE

We cannot change what we do not first accept.

How do we start the process of feeling good when the shit keeps hitting the fan? For me, the first step is acceptance, the second is more acceptance, and the third is even deeper acceptance. My running joke helps me not get stuck in the stubbornness of nonacceptance, which usually happens when the shame of "I am not enough" attacks from my ego-mind.

More than 2,500 years ago, Buddha focused an entire spiritual movement on the concept of non-attachment. He taught it as the key to ending craving

> "And acceptance is the answer to all my problems today."
> *~Alcoholics Anonymous, fourth edition*

and its resulting suffering by encouraging his followers to accept life in the moment. We must acknowledge the reality of the present moment before we try to change it.

Buddha's message is when we don't practice acceptance, we suffer. Knowing this helps me remember the importance of compassion when I make mistakes, think others don't like me or feel insecure. Keeping life in the now is vital to letting go of our resistance.

Acceptance is how we begin to unravel and address our issue—first, through an admission, then acceptance, followed by action if it's necessary.

Acceptance, one of the simplest and most profound practices I know, allows us to understand that we don't have to know how things will turn out. We don't have to make assumptions or predictions about what will happen in the future. Our assumptions and projections are often untrue, and we end up distrusting life. We might even believe we are trusting, but our anxiety, actions, and reactions tell a different story.

We must let go of control outside ourselves, or we will never know inner peace and trust life or ourselves. The caterpillar does not cling to his old garment and thus transforms into a magnificent butterfly. The caterpillar trusts his maker and that all is well. Everything is in a constant state of change. When we fight change or try to hold onto life, people, places, and things, we suffer greatly. To trust is to allow the Universal Power to look after the outcome.

∞

What Stops Us From Letting Go?

We become high-jacked by our painful emotions when we attach our identity to the pain and forget there is no permanence in any emotion. Our solution: we let the feeling [fully] in; so we can let it [fully] go.

Think of an impatient mother demanding that her clinging child let go.

> "All you are asked to do is let it in."
> -A Course in Miracles

The more she insists the child stop, the more her child hangs on. Only when she takes a deep breath, composes herself, and asks from a compassionate, understanding, and loving place will her child begin to loosen their grip.

The mother - lets in [acceptance and love], and her baby finally lets go.

Another example: A man ends his relationship with his wife but the wife wants to cling and not let go. She suffers beyond belief. It is not until she lets in that it's over, can she then begin to let it go.

Beginning in childhood, all I saw were my faults and imperfections, not my gifts. I

> Life is a continuous letting go. There is no permanence.

thought my unique personality was flawed. Being a stubborn lad, I decided to show my father, friends, and the world how lovable and memorable I was. I went out into the world, determined to be whomever I needed to be to fit in. I didn't know that I wouldn't feel accepted by others if I didn't accept myself. When I let go of seeking outside myself, the right people started to show up in my life to embrace my uniqueness as I would embrace theirs. It was challenging in the beginning. I had to catch myself when I found I was trying to change myself to fit in.

We all have shortcomings. Recognizing that this is part of being human took away a lot of my shame, self-judgment, and comparing myself to others. It allowed me to begin the vital work of unconditional self-acceptance.

I committed to treating myself with kindness, unconditional self-compassion, and self-acceptance to the best of my ability. Love blossomed in this fertile soil, and I began to stop blaming and criticizing myself. I also committed to only having close relationships with people who knew and fully accepted the real me.

To fully accept ourselves, we must courageously acknowledge the harm we've done to ourselves and others. We must be willing to share all of our darkness with someone we trust to be free of it. Without the practice of unconditional self-acceptance, I wouldn't have been able to look at myself objectively, forgive myself

> "A certain darkness is needed to see the stars."[22]
> ~Osho, mystic, founder of the Rajneesh movement

and others, and become my best friend.

This compassion allowed me to accept my human self, with all its imperfections, in one hand and my divine self in the other. I was able to silence the voice of self-judgment and begin to live authentically.

∞

The Critical Voice

The critical voice whispers the compulsive, destructive thoughts that block our recovery, spiritual growth, emotional intelligence, and joy for life. Another name for this voice of self-judgment is the *superego*. Would you be friends with anyone who said the negative shit we tell ourselves? No, of course not!

Judgment arises automatically in our minds. We didn't decide we will judge ourselves or others. We are not doing it deliberately. Our mind is doing it. Hence, we take responsibility - not by not having judgments, and definitely not by telling ourselves, we shouldn't be judgmental. Instead – we notice the judgment and get curious about it by asking questions.

What parts of me do I not accept, and liked about myself?

What is the underlying belief, and when did that belief get started?

So our judgments are not bad things, they're guides to where we are still resenting and rejecting ourselves. Get curious. Be the observer. It was how we developed greater compassion for ourselves.

Comparing myself and clean time to others used to be one of my favorite self-punishments that provided me an excuse to continue to self-medicate. It took years of self-awareness to stop the insanity of the superego and its self-destructive patterns. Today I understand that the critical voices are just like any of our thoughts, just like birds chirping in a tree, clouds floating by in the sky, the wind rustling the leaves, or cars passing on a busy freeway. They have no permanence as long as we let go of our resistance and belief that thoughts are who we are.

I could not have done it without the help from my mentors, friends in recovery, and myself to recognize when I would fall into the old pattern of putting myself down.

∞

Love Begins With Us

If you didn't receive the nurturing you needed or still wrestle with a self-critical voice, look in the mirror each morning for the next thirty days, and repeat this mirror affirmation that you've taped on your mirror:

> "I love you (your name). I love you. I am a beautiful
> soul. I am smart. I am worthy of the very best in life.
> There has never been and never will be anyone like
> me. I will be vulnerable. I will speak from the heart
> and stay humble. I will be my best friend. I will
> practice compassion and loving-kindness for myself.
> I am enough. I am more than enough, and I will
> always be enough. Now get to work (your name).
> The world needs you!"

Write the above affirmation on a piece of paper each evening about thirty minutes before going to bed. Completing both exercises is essential to reprogramming your subconscious mind and creating a new loving relationship with yourself through daily action.

To further help break the pattern of putting myself down, I carried a picture of me as an innocent kid to re-parent little Paul. Each time I caught myself in self-condemnation, I would look at the picture on my phone and confirm that I was good enough. I repeated this for one year, and it did wonders for breaking the stronghold of my critical voice.

Remember, the superego is not our enemy, just old programming. Instead, become curious and compassionate with the critical voice and knowing it's not who we are.

> Learn more with my video, The Turnaround. https://youtu.be/wjsy KnlluHU

∞

Self-Forgiveness: the Practice of Unconditional Self-Acceptance

Understanding that my addiction and mistaken identity were behind my inability to forgive myself made it much easier to let go and practice self-forgiveness in recovery.

The following quote further expanded and enhanced my self-forgiveness.

Only the ego and toxic shame of our mistaken identity stop us from knowing all is forgiven at all times because God does not know condemnation. The only thing holding us back from being forgiven is ourselves.

> "The Source (God) does not know forgiveness because God is Love, and God cannot forgive because IT has never condemned."
> -A Course in Miracles

As part of my healing process, I wrote down on paper the things that I had not been able to forgive myself for, attaching the "I forgive you …" to each. Then, I said the words out loud: "I forgive you for not finishing university. I forgive you for stealing from Linda. I forgive you for introducing Nicole to cocaine. I forgive you for abandoning Tiny. I forgive you for being dishonest with your family over many years of addiction. I forgive you for cheating on your ex-wife. I forgive you for trying to kill yourself."

Next, I shared these and my deepest secrets with another trusted human being. In the twelve-step world, this is part of step five.

Forgiving ourselves does not mean that we condone or minimize behaviors where we may have harmed others. It's about understanding and accepting that we are human

> Continuing sobriety is one of the most important living amends we can make to the people we've hurt.

beings who make mistakes. If amends are called for, we make them.

Forgiving Others

When we forgive others, we do not condone their hurtful actions or behaviors. We let go of our resentment, anger, and rage towards the other person to move on with our lives. The alternative is more constriction, loss of freedom, and painful relationships.

I forgave my father when I finally saw how my unwillingness to forgive him harmed me and discovered the horrible things he suffered in his childhood. It made perfect sense why my father treated me the way he did. One of my favorite forgiveness quotes comes from biblical Jesus on the cross, saying, "Forgive them Father for they don't know what they do." It helped me recognize that Dad treated me wrongly because he was unconsciously operating from his unresolved past. It opened my heart to more profound forgiveness.

In the process of forgiving him, I had to forgive myself for taking all that had happened so overwhelmingly personal.

Forgiveness is about choosing compassion and not allowing the past to define us. When we give up trying to settle scores and

> Forgiveness is the gift you give to yourself.

surrender to the Universal Mind and its Karma, we find peace.

None of us know the process within the spiritual realm and its impact on our future. Knowing that Love is our final destination because we are Love already will help you with deeper acceptance and forgiveness.

∞

A Declaration of Commitment to Truth, Love, and Peace

"I let go of all reasons and excuses for not accepting myself. I will practice unconditional self-acceptance as a way of life."

HEALING PRINCIPLE 6

TRUST

Trust makes recovery possible.

Every addicted person has trust issues. Its absence leaves us in a state of anxiety and confusion, making it difficult for us to ask for help, heal our broken hearts, undo the attached shame, and access the One Power of Love, Peace, and Joy.

Our distrust comes from the loss of connection to our authentic selves. In my case, the essential parent-child trust bond was never well established. I became a little boy who believed that it must be my fault if something went wrong. I didn't trust myself. I learned to fake trusting others to avoid consequences. This unwillingness to trust became part of my mistaken identity and kept me sick in the disease of addiction.

∞

Learning to Trust

Before I could learn trust, I had to continue practicing *not* trusting myself in early recovery because I still wanted drugs and alcohol. I had to let go absolutely, to trust others and reach out for help.

I eventually learned to trust by becoming aware of when I wasn't trusting. I had to take my hands off the steering wheel and humbly ask the universe and people in recovery to show me a new way to live.

I began to trust myself when I committed doing the next right thing.

∞

Trust=Love

Trust is the key to a personal relationship with Love (God). We can only know the One Power through a trusting relationship with ourselves.

Christian author Rick Warren wrote, "You will never know God is all you need until God is all you have."

> "Learn to trust the journey, even when you do not understand it."
> ~Lolly Daskal, executive leadership coach, speaker, Lead From Within founder

I came to know this intimately while being held in remand at Toronto's Don Jail from January to December 2007.

∞

The Don Jail

After another relapse, I had lost everything again, including my girlfriend of two years. I was in my apartment, waiting patiently for a government check. It was supposed to cover my first and last month's rent, but I had a different plan—use the money for a life-ending cocaine overdose. I reasoned that no one would know it was a suicide if I killed myself this way. Those in recovery know that using is slow suicide. It's often hard to tell if an overdose results from a slow suicide or an intentional one.

While I was waiting for the mail, my doorbell rang. One of the two men outside asked if I would let them in to see one of the units for rent. After I let them in, they asked if I was Paul Noiles.

Before I knew it, they handcuffed me, read my rights, and arrested me for bank robbery.

I wasn't worried about the charge since I'd never robbed a bank. I was most concerned about the delay in getting high and ending my life. I was sure they would take me to the police station, clear it up, and I'd be back home in a few hours. Instead, I spent the next eleven and a half months in remand at the overcrowded, filthy, gang-run Don Jail. It was not my first time at the Don, but it was the longest and the only time I was one hundred percent innocent of the crime. However, my family, friends, and lawyer believed otherwise because I was considered a flight risk and denied bail due to seven outstanding shoplifting charges I had left behind in Vancouver. I felt utterly powerless.

The remand unit in any jail is a dangerous place. It holds people accused of rape, murder, arson, sex crimes, robbery, and other crimes, who are waiting to appear before the courts. While at the Don, I saw violence, racism, drug use, and a guy hang himself in his cell. I was broken, alone, and lost. Faced with the realization that no one was coming to save me, I decided to surrender.

I had suffered many relapses over the previous ten years, but I had also done much spiritual work. Now I was being called to trust and have faith at an entirely new level. I went through many painful days of trusting and not trusting. The fire of discomfort slowly revealed a beautiful soul.

After seven months in custody, I was in a holding cell, waiting to go to court for a pre-trial hearing. I meditated and asked my Higher Power for help, waiting patiently for guidance. Suddenly, I felt as if a gentle wind had caressed me. I heard a mighty voice reassuring me, telling me that I had nothing to worry about, that I wouldn't be found guilty. The voice encouraged me not to plead guilty to something I didn't do, to trust, and to know that All is Well.

At the courthouse, I entered a small holding room to talk with my lawyer. He explained that the Crown offered me a sixteen-month sentence if I changed my plea to guilty. The court would be credit me two days for each day I had already served in pre-trial custody, and they would release me in thirty days. However, if found guilty, I would be looking at a four- to five-year federal sentence. Remembering the message from my Higher Power, I said, "No, they can go fuck themselves. I'm innocent. I won't plead guilty to something I didn't do."

Four months later, I was acquitted and walked away, a free man.

∞

A Declaration of Commitment to Truth, Love, and Peace

"All is well, and I am safe. I will trust in the power of Love to heal and guide me in all ways. I will believe in the process of life."

HEALING PRINCIPLE 7

FAITH

꒰◦ ◦꒱

Faith is the knowledge that there is nothing to fear.

꒰◦ ◦꒱

The true meaning of faith is being in the flow of life and, in doing so, finding that life tends to cooperate with us. When we have faith, everything works in unity because we connect to and trust life itself. Trust and faith work in sync with each other.

Letting go of the illusion of control was how I began to develop great faith. But I had to approach faith slowly and with an open mind because of my trust issues. The process started with focusing on my body—how my lungs were breathing for me, my heart pumping blood, all keeping keep me alive without any conscious effort on my part. It made sense to me that a Higher Power (Universal Intelligence) must be doing the same for every sentient being.

From a trust base, I could expand my faith into other parts of life and human experience, including nature. For example, if it weren't for trees, we wouldn't have oxygen and hence, no me or you. If not for insects, we would no longer exist. Without the sun at the perfect distance from the earth, life may not have begun or continue to flourish. I believe the One Power runs

> "Faith is trust. Faith is a deep sense of connectedness with Being."
>
> ~Eckhart Tolle, spiritual leader, author

through everything that exists. It holds all substances together. It is the energy of existence itself—a loving power for good purpose.

Faith within the precepts of organized religion works for many, but it isn't the only way to acquire a belief system for divining universal truth. While the truth is simple, seeking the truth is complex. Our fears, past programming, family dysfunction, distrust of authority, unhealthy motivations, and the mistaken belief that we need power and control can hide the truth.

We can only know the One Power in the Universe through ourselves; no one can do it for us. As Reverend Lorraine once said, "As we evolve, so will our ideas of God." In other words, Spirit is always changing because we are ever-evolving. If you want a better life, open yourself to different ideas of Source (God). When we cultivate faith in our daily activities, goodwill begins to manifest in our lives.

The more we practice faith, the more freedom we experience. Simple acts of faith have amazing power. Even if you only give 10 percent of yourself in faith and action, the One Power (God) will provide the other 90 percent.

Repetitively saying the simple mantra "Trust Life, Trust Love, Trust Source (God)" has saved me many times, pulling me out of my ego-self and returning me to inner peace and trust.

> "The kingdom of heaven is like a mustard seed, which a man took and planted in his field. Though it is the smallest of all seeds, when it grows, it is the largest of garden plants and becomes a tree, so that the birds come and perch in its branches."
> ~Matthew 13:31-32

Every bit of my story is a story of faith. Despite relapses, near-death experiences, loss of loved ones, suicide attempts, homelessness, and jail time, I never gave up.

∞

If someone had told me years ago that two detectives would play an essential part in my faith and recovery, I would have laughed.

April 20, 2013

I woke up every day in my apartment at a government-funded building in Toronto disgusted, penniless, and owing money to one or more drug dealers. I then spent the rest of my day stealing expensive liquor bottles to sell to restaurants, bars, and pawn shops. Every day, I told myself that I'd pay off my dealers and not buy more crack.

As I was getting ready to smoke crack, I heard a knock at my door. I looked out the peephole and saw what looked like two detectives. After I asked what they wanted, one of them said they had a warrant for my arrest and to open the door. When I asked for what, the detective continued, "We have you on camera stealing booze at six liquor stores in downtown Toronto. Open the door!" I asked them to slide the warrant under the door, guessing they didn't have one and couldn't legally come in. As I continued to smoke crack, I talked with them on the other side of the door. They left and a few hours later, returned and slid the warrant under the door.

Paranoia took hold, and I decided to end my life. I opened the window of my ninth-floor apartment and stepped out on the ledge—the fear was overpowering. Pissed at myself for not having the courage to jump, I started to cry, went back inside, and unlocked the door. I was sure the detectives would give me a good beating, but, instead, they handcuffed me and put me in the back of their unmarked car.

Overwhelmed with disgust, I once again went into withdrawal in a cold, concrete holding cell. A short time later, Detective Lauren Hassard came by and handed me a picture she'd found of me online winning the Mr. Ottawa Bodybuilding contest. "This is who you really are, right?" she asked. Detective Wayne Fowler showed up a short time later. He kindly said, "You're not a bad person, Paul, just very ill."

After my sentencing, I found out that Detective Hassard had a close friend who had died of a heroin overdose, and Detective Fowler had family and friends who suffered from addictions. They both understood I was more than my addiction and chose to witness the light within me. I could have gone to jail for a long time, but the two detectives and my lawyer, Blair, advocated on my behalf. I received a sentence of a three-month

> My lawyer was Blair Drummie, an old friend from our years together at the University of New Brunswick. Blair represented me every time I was arrested, and he did it all pro bono (no payment). Thank you, Blair! I will be forever grateful.

house arrest with significant stipulations. I'm still friends with both detectives today. The compassion they showed me changed my life.

I Am Not My Criminal Record

I never wanted or planned to be a criminal. All I cared about was getting the next hit after years of addiction. I had lost all self-respect and didn't care about the consequences.

I was arrested for the first time when I was thirty-six years old. I had stints anywhere from two to seven days, thirty to ninety days, five months, and eleven and a half months, a total of seventeen incarcerations. Ninety-five percent of the charges were for shoplifting.

I didn't have to share my criminal record, and some will think I am crazy for exposing it. I did it to support and comfort others who are still living in shame for their criminal past. It took a long time to recognize that my crimes and criminal records did not define me. As Sister Helen Prejean says, "People are more than the worst thing they have ever done in their lives."

What does define us is what we do with our lives after we take full responsibility. Shame is dangerous in recovery, and we must forgive ourselves before healing can begin.

∞

A Declaration of Commitment to Truth, Love, and Peace

"I have faith that everything in my life is working for my highest good. The Universe naturally and freely provides for all my needs."

SECTION D

THE SEVEN PRACTICES OF AWAKENING

There can be no awakening of consciousness if we are not willing to change our daily routines. Trying new practices and consistently using them is how we reprogram our subconscious mind, dismantle our mistaken identity, and stop relapsing.

AWAKENING PRACTICE 1

RECOVERY MEETINGS

*I would not have survived if I had relied entirely
on the twelve-step recovery program, but I
would not have succeeded without it.*

A woman enters a dark room and lights a small candle to alleviate her anxiety. The candle's light dissolves some of the room's darkness, and the woman's anxiety subsides a little, but the space remains relatively dark. A man then walks in and lights his candle, adding more light to the room. Both feel more at ease. Then, another person enters and lights their candle, then another, and another, and another, and another. The glowing candles of several people now provide abundant light for everyone in the room. The collective group of candles represents One Love.

The light analogy is how I see the support meetings worldwide. The One Love is all around the room. Even if we are incapable of receiving the love, our body will never forget it, and healing can begin.

We can do together what we cannot do alone.

The light represents the importance of human connection, especially when experiencing addiction's darkness. We have a hard time seeing ourselves objectively when alone in our pain and suffering. We all have blindsides. Without the light of human connection, it's impossible to recover.

When you feel blinded, reach for the light. Call a mentor, a sponsor, or someone you trust. Attend a recovery meeting.

Whatever life throws at us—death, divorce, financial ruin, poverty, homelessness, unemployment, cancer, illness, jail—it doesn't matter. It's easier to get through anything when we stay clean and sober and reach out to other light bearers.

I had to become willing to let go of my pride, fear, shame, and arrogance and, with humble vulnerability, I reached out and asked for help.

I went to my first twelve-step meeting in 1991 because I was in pain from the consequences of addiction, not because I wanted to stop. However, like the many other people who have yet to accept their addiction, those early meetings informed me I could no longer deny I had a problem. Acceptance and surrender would still be a long way off, yet the seeds of recovery were planted.

> The inability to reach out for help, according to some research, is a leading reason for relapse.

I met other people who shared similar stories at meetings, walked the same path, faced the same day-to-day struggles. I was not alone. If they could do it, surely I could. I began to develop hope that recovery was possible.

∞

Other Fellowships

A 2012 report on addiction treatment in the U.S. by the National Center on Addiction and Substance Abuse[23] at Columbia University stated, " The research evidence demonstrates that a one-size-fits-all approach to addiction treatment typically is a recipe for failure."

The research also showed the success rate of those attending twelve-step alternative recovery groups, such as *Smart Recovery, Recovery Dharma, Refuge Recovery, Secular Organizations for*

Sobriety, and Celebrate Recovery, is much the same.[24] There is also a growing list of online recovery support groups. *She Recovers* an inspiring group of strong and courageous women coming together in recovery. *In the Rooms* is a website with online meetings for most every fellowship known to man.

Recovery groups offer meetings that focus on connection, healing, and recovery every single day of the year. It's a great way

> *Try different recovery groups. Attend at least ten meetings before deciding which ones are a good fit.*

to begin to reprogram the subconscious mind.

While millions of people have achieved long-term recovery by working the steps with a sponsor and participating in the fellowship, some may need a different approach. A large percentage may also require additional help from outside sources.

Often when a person relapses, they feel not only the pain of letting themselves down but the shame of letting down their friends in the fellowship. As I did, many people who have relapsed stay away from meetings for an extended period

> "Don't let the twelve steps become your life. Get a life because of the twelve steps."
> ~Tommy Rosen, yoga teacher, Recovery 2.0 founder

because of embarrassment and ego attachment. I also had a few friends who never came back to meetings. Some of them died. A focus on counting clean or sober time can contribute to this.

Our biggest challenge with a relapse is our mistaken identity trying to convince us not to come back. It plays right into the negative narrative that we are failures. This sense of loss can often be heightened because of the subtle (or not-so-subtle) message from a support group that we weren't working the steps hard enough because if we were, we wouldn't have relapsed. Even if it's valid, criticism and judgment are useless; compassion is what people need most. If you have shame, share it with your sponsor or someone you trust. It's what I had to do.

You'll find in the rooms, just as anywhere in life, uncompassionate, arrogant, and judgmental people. There will always be people who piss us off at the meetings. They give us a glorious opportunity to learn how to deal with conflict and personalities.

Back in the day, when I was still carrying the heavy load of toxic shame, I often relapsed right after attending someone's recovery birthday celebration. All my program friends were celebrating birthdays—one, two, three, four years—but I couldn't put together a single year of continuous sobriety. It became another great excuse to use.

The thing to remember is that most people in the rooms of recovery will love you right where you are. To witness healing—love moving back and forth between people as they bare their souls at a meeting—is a marvelous thing.

All my closest friends have come out of the recovery rooms, and I would not have made it without them. They have all enriched my life. I continue to find treasures, great and small spiritual insights from newcomers and others, and the opportunity to be of service.

Each person with an addiction is a unique, complex human being who has to find a recovery program that works for them.

A.A. meetings convene in approximately 180 nations worldwide, with a membership estimated at more than two million members. More than 70,000 Narcotics Anonymous meetings assemble in 144 countries, and many other twelve-step fellowships around the world facilitate recovery for individuals with addiction.

∞

Many Roads to Recovery

Kenny was one of the most surprising persons with an addiction I have ever met. He was an active member of a twelve-step program but could not stay clean. His recovery friends blamed him for his relapses. Kenny stopped going to meetings and got involved with his local church. Eventually, he had a spiritual awakening at church and lost all desire to use. He is now ten years clean.

Bob Mariner, a recovery coach in Canada, found his recovery at Secular Organizations for Sobriety, also known as Save Our Selves. It's a non-profit network of autonomous addiction recovery groups that are not religious or spiritual in nature. They don't see spirituality or surrendering to a Higher Power as necessary to maintaining abstinence. The suggested guidelines of SOS emphasize rational decision-making.

Having a recovery support group, the twelve steps, and compassionate people in the rooms, especially in the beginning, were an essential part of my holistic program of recovery. Fellowships are about we; one person with an addiction helping another without expecting anything in exchange. I am a better person when I support new and returning people.

Going through recovery alone is not a wise decision. Try to think of recovery meetings as a mastermind group, a place of higher learning.

∞

A Declaration of Commitment to Truth, Love, and Peace

"I will keep an open mind when it comes to recovery meetings. I will make wise decisions based on the experience of people I trust and respect. I will follow the truth to the best of my ability. The truth shall set me free."

AWAKENING PRACTICE 2

MEDITATION AND MINDFULNESS

*When you can be OK in complete silence,
you will be OK with yourself.*

An addiction counselor told me in 1999 that he wished he could lock me alone in a quiet room for six months, so I could make peace with myself. I thought he was nuts, but I later wondered if the only way I would even know true peace was if I spent quality time by myself in silence. Since silence activated the pain of not liking who I thought I was, I thought it was worth checking out.

Obsessive-compulsive thinking is a significant component of addiction. Each morning I woke up and began obsessively thinking of ways and means to continue to use.

> "Silence is the absolute core of reality; the inner nature of all that is."
> ~Swami Premodaya, spiritual master, International Centers of Divine Awakening founder

I tried many ways to fix my thinking problem, everything from positive thinking, gratitude, and prayer, but nothing worked. Why? Because we can't resolve thinking problems with more thought. We must first learn slow down our thinking (meditation) before learning to think consciously.

Meditation is exercise for the thinking mind. In meditation, we are not trying to change our experience. We are changing our relationship to our experience. Meditation is about being Awareness, *not* about being aware.

Meditation was how I first experienced that I was not the thoughts and feelings of my mind or the lies of my mistaken identity. I also began to experience the eternal silence of All that Is, another name for God. In the silence and stillness

> If you're working on the twelve steps of recovery, don't wait for step eleven to practice meditation. You'll find its benefits, even if you meditate each day for just five minutes.

of meditation, I would eventually find a state of complete connectedness with all life by experiencing "I Am"—which has nothing to do with any identity.

Meditation is a holy state that changes our perceptions of ourselves and others. The more we practice it, the more we wake up to our magnificence and the same splendor in others and life.

I used to find meditation difficult but kept trying. I researched the works of the greatest minds and found most of them practiced a morning meditation ritual.

> "Meditation is not an escape from life ... but preparation for really being in life."
> ~Thich Nhat Hanh, Zen master, writer, poet, scholar, peacemaker

It was the motivation I needed to continue developing a daily meditation practice. I understood that I had to learn how to meditate or continue to live in misery.

The answers to all our questions lie waiting in the Silent Intelligence that permeates the whole universe, not in more thinking, talk therapy, or book knowledge.

∞

Consciousness

Thinking and consciousness (awareness) are not the same. Thought cannot exist without consciousness, but consciousness can exist without thought. We don't contain the consciousness. The consciousness contains us.

Consciousness is the foundation of all because it precedes everything, and it is the primary factor in creation. Action is the second factor in the manifestation process.

Consciousness uses the mind, experiences, thoughts, feelings, and body sensations. When I realized "I am Consciousness," my perception of reality shifted profoundly. No one can be awake without daily spiritual practice that helps them recognize consciousness.

∞

Being

I had to learn just to be. I had to have an intimate relationship with Being, or there would be no

> "Love is a state of Being."
> ~Eckhart Tolle, spiritual leader, author

recovery or letting go of my mistaken identity. That same Being is in every one of us. It is the inextinguishable flame whose presence is eternal. It is the light that would not let me give up—written into the energetic code of our spiritual DNA. Being is our most loyal companion, willing to wait forever until we pay attention.

∞

Breath is Essential for Life

When we are upset, resentful, angry, anxious, or fearful, our breathing becomes rapid and shallow. Our heart may beat a little faster, our blood pressure may increase, and our sympathetic nervous system triggers the body's ancient fight-or-flight response. By applying a deep breathing technique, we can shift our current emotions to one of peace.

Breath is fundamental: My lungs breathe for me—it just happens. I don't have to think about it. I breathe! In other words, something bigger than me must be doing it for me. What a revelation, knowing when I focus on breath, I am aware of my oneness with Source. I can affirm that our life goes well whenever we are aware of oneness with Source.

> Let your breath be the anchor when feeling overwhelmed. Pause, take a deep breath, and let it guide you.

There are many variations of breathing *exercises*. I like to use the five-five breath: breathe in through the nose for a count of five, hold for five, then breathe out through the nose for a count of five. Repeat until you feel relaxed and grounded.

Breath of Fire and Ego Eradicator are also some of my favorite breathing exercises that you can find on YouTube. Try these and explore others.

Regular daily practice of deep breathing is a simple tool for improving our health and emotional well-being, supporting our lasting recovery.

> "This is why I call breath a game-changer: it literally changes everything in your experience once you start to practice."
> -Tommy Rosen, yoga teacher, Recovery 2.0 founder

∞

The Science Behind Meditation

Science shows that daily meditation is effective for addiction because it rewires critical pathways in the brain. A study on mindfulness[25] assessed people who meditated daily for thirty minutes over eight weeks. The result was that the subjects increased the brain's gray matter associated with learning, memory, self-awareness, introspection, and decreased areas linked to anxiety and stress.

Studies from the Exploration of Consciousness Research Institute, better known as EOC Institute, found:[26]

- Meditation stimulates and trains the brain to be naturally high without the need for alcohol, marijuana, drugs, cigarettes, or any other addictive substance.
- Meditation supercharges the brain and body with endorphins, super-pleasurable natural brain hormones. The meditator's high is more potent than that of the well-known runner's high.
- A landmark 2002 study at the John F. Kennedy Institute found that 65 percent of subjects boosted their dopamine levels during meditation. The levels remained at an optimally healthy range when they were not meditating.
- In a 2006 study at the University of Washington, researchers examined seventy-eight prison inmates with a substance addiction. While in prison, they were taught how to meditate for ten days. After leaving jail, they self-reported their substance use for over ninety days. The study found that of the inmates who continued to practice meditation, 87 percent used less alcohol, and 89 percent used less marijuana. Furthermore, meditation was almost six times more effective than the control group's more traditional chemical dependency treatment plan.

Meditation transforms the central nervous system and brain, shifting the body chemistry out of fight-or-flight survival mode. It's a natural pain killer and one of the best ways to naturally change body chemistry.

∞

Warm-up Before Meditation

Just as runners stretch before running, those who meditate benefit greatly from a warm-up. Here arc a few ways I did that.

Chakra Breathing: Focus on your seven chakras, one at a time, as if each chakra is breathing on its own. Begin with the crown chakra, then descend and visualize each chakra opening as the golden light of *prana* (Hindu for life-giving force) enters during the in-breath, and the light leaves through the out-breath. I do three breath cycles for each of the seven chakras, one after another. It will draw you out of your head and into your body and make your transition into meditation easier.

A *mantra* is a word, words, or sounds repeated until the mind gets bored and naturally slows down. It's a great way to prepare for meditation. You can use a simple mantra such as, "I am love, peace, and joy" or "I am not my body, not even my mind." Repetition is essential.

Full-Body Tensing. It involves squeezing and holding each muscle for a few seconds and then releasing them. Begin with the toes, then move up to your calves, thighs, hamstrings, butt, abs, and face, then finally contract the whole body all at once, then release.

> Mala beads are similar to rosaries. They help keep the focus on repetitive prayer. I say my mantra once for each of the 108 beads. The number's significance is open to interpretation, but 108 has long been considered a sacred number in Hinduism and yoga. Renowned mathematicians of Vedic culture see it as a number of the wholeness of existence.

Each person must find the techniques that work best for them. However, every teacher I've studied with promotes reaching the no-mind through complete stillness and silence while focusing on the breath and observing thoughts without attachment.

∞

Self-Inquiry

I've been practicing self-inquiry after discovering the Indian philosopher Jiddu Krishnamurti's work ten years ago. Self-inquiry has led me to higher dimensions of reality and truth. Because meditation puts me in a heightened state of consciousness, I usually do self-inquiry afterward.

Meditation is about stillness, silence, and a state of being. Self-Inquiry is a bold, fearless questioning of our being and discerning the answers. It is about challenging our beliefs, thoughts, judgments, opinions, and interpretations to discern false from truth. It's about kicking the ego to the curb whenever it tries to enter the conversation. The idea is to slowly and deliberately question and investigate.

We ask our questions in silence and wait patiently for the answer without jumping to conclusions or assumptions. We do not answer it with our minds. We wait for Being to provide the solution. Self-inquiry has been a critical tool in my spiritual awakening.

> "To hold a question inwardly in silent and patient waiting is an art rarely mastered these days. Inquiry is a bridge between the ego and the soul, and beyond to the Infinite."[27]
> —Adyashanti, spiritual teacher, author

Some of the questions I've asked include: "Am I thoughts? Am I feelings? Am I the body?" "What is addiction? Am I an addict? Who is the addict?" "Who is experiencing these thoughts, feelings, and body sensations? Is there anything here besides thoughts, feelings, body sensations?" "Why do I have a belief? Who taught me this belief? How did I learn this belief?" "What is awareness? Am I awareness? Where is awareness? Who is experiencing awareness? Can I find myself in awareness?"

I listen for the answer and usually hear it. I ask myself if the answer is from the ego or higher consciousness. The answer is often completely different from what I had previously thought. It's how I know it's coming from Source or Higher Power.

After years of self-inquiry, I have experienced non-duality and *no-self*, the possibility of there being no "me" or "you" or "others," that everything is Oneness. The most incredible illusion in the world is the belief that we are separate selves. When I discovered the opposite, it changed everything. I finally understood what all the mystics meant when they said that if we hurt anyone, we wound our self.

∞

What Is Mindfulness?

We practice mindfulness by maintaining a moment-by-moment awareness of our thoughts, feelings, bodily sensations, and the surrounding environment. We focus as an observer and allow our thoughts to unfold without judgment or attachment.

Mindfulness is a form of meditation. Jon Kabat-Zinn, founding executive director of Mindfulness in Medicine, Health Care, and Society, defines meditation as "the awareness that arises from paying attention, on purpose, in the present moment and non-judgmentally." Mindfulness practice begins when we focus on breathing, walking, observing nature, drinking coffee, or even washing dishes. When we wash dishes mindfully, we pay close attention to the job at hand. We don't get lost in resentments about being the only one in the house who does dishes.

For a simple, mindful, breath-focused meditation, sit quietly and comfortably with a straight spine. Close your eyes. Make it your intention to be open and in the moment. Now bring your attention to your breath. Notice as you slowly inhale and exhale. Observe what is naturally taking place. If your mind begins to wander, as it inevitably will, notice this and gently bring your attention back to your breath. Judging your thoughts is like quicksand. Struggling will only make you sink more quickly.

Try this meditation for five minutes. Build up to twenty minutes a day if you can. It's better to practice mindfulness for a few minutes a day than not at all.[28]

YouTube has many mindfulness meditation videos. I especially like Jon Kabat-Zinn's body-scan meditations. Find the ones you enjoy.

∞

Silent Power

Silent power is a practice that teaches us not to react when we sense criticism, attack, false accusation, or judgment. Instead, we practice silence and do nothing. Silent power allows us an opportunity to observe and determine what belief is triggered and determine what is real and false.

My big ego, in combination with my hypersensitivity, made Silent Power initially challenging to learn. Still, I knew I wouldn't grow up emotionally until I learned to do nothing and sit with my discomfort. The more I practiced silent power, the more I discovered how most of my suffering was an illusion.

We often believe we have made conscious choices when, in reality, our subconscious mind is behind our overreactions. Studies from the 1970s demonstrate that our brains prepare for action just over a third of a second before we consciously decide to act. The subconscious mind cannot move outside its fixed programs—it automatically reacts to situations from its stored behavior responses.

> Meditation is a deeper form of silence that not only saved my life; it freed me from the bondage of self.

Most of the time, we're not aware that we are acting unconsciously.

Silent power gave me breathing room. I developed greater access to a higher state of consciousness with repetition and practice, which overwrote many of my old limiting subconscious beliefs.

∞

A Declaration of Commitment to Truth, Love, and Peace

"I will practice daily meditation each day. It changes my relationship to who and what I am."

AWAKENING PRACTICE 3

PRAYER AND GRATITUDE

Show me a grateful person in recovery and I will show you a person who is not using their substance or behavior of choice.

In 2010, after telling Reverend Lorraine about the resentments I still had towards my father, she suggested I make a list of my good and bad childhood memories, then call her when I was ready to share. To my amazement, the good memories list was longer than the bad!

Reverend Lorraine then recommended that I then use affirmative prayer as a spiritual treatment for my resentments with Dad.

Each morning I would bring Dad into my consciousness, seeing him as whole and healthy, complete in mind, body, and spirit. I would see him as love, peace, and joy, fully connected and One with God. If my thoughts strayed, I would return to my intention not to judge, but to see him as Spirit sees him, ending with "And So It Is!"

After three years of daily affirmation and prayer, the phone rang Christmas morning. I thought it was Mom calling to wish me a

> "Prayer does not change God, but it changes him who prays."
> ~Sören Kierkegaard, Danish philosopher

Merry Christmas, but, for the first time in eighteen years, it was Dad calling me! Our conversation was brief, but it gave me hope.

I continued to pray, and, three years later, he phoned to wish me a happy birthday. Not perfection, but progress.

I continued affirmative prayer. Two years later, I flew home to see my family for the first time in twenty-three years.

∞

Trip Home

I had many mixed emotions as I prepared to board my flight with my little dog Sharona:

Nervously thinking about hugging my seventy-eight-year-old Dad and saying, I love you. Seeing my baby sister Lana and meeting her husband and son, Luke, for the first time. Connecting with older brother Dave, his wife Judy, and grown sons Tyler and Drew, who never had an opportunity to know their uncle. And to wrap my arms around Mom.

I was joyfully surprised that Dad came with Mom to pick me up at the airport. The next morning, Mom told me her dream had come true when she heard Dad and me laughing in the living room. The next day we played Family Feud at Lana's house. When asked what a cowboy would ride if he didn't have a horse, Mom answered, "Another cowboy!" We all laughed.

We went to my brother's house the following day, where I had a private conversation with Drew and Tyler. I made amends for not being there for them and shared a little about my painful addiction years and now in long-term recovery, helping those who still suffer. They shared their fear and sadness of not knowing if they would ever see their uncle again. We had an emotional hug. It was a wonderful healing moment.

Learn more by viewing my video, Gratitude.
https://youtu.be/hxBAQBEIcGY

The trip was full of healing, insight, and wisdom. It reconfirmed that I was doing what Spirit had always intended, loving my life and my family.

However, after boarding the jet for home, I began to feel angry about Dad's staring straight ahead and not responding when I tried to have a conversation about the last 23 years of my life. I was reacting like a child, feeling unheard and inadequate, filled with shame, and too afraid to ask why he wasn't answering me.

Over the next thirty days, I searched every crevice of my soul with my mentor Reverend Lorraine and Reverend Liz. After lots of reflection and self-inquiry, it became apparent that my anger was not at Dad. I was angry at myself. You see, I'd forgiven Dad many times throughout my life, but I still carried the same unrealistic expectations of a loving father-son relationship that I'd had since I was a kid. I had to accept that Art didn't want to talk about the past or his feelings. He couldn't give me the love and support I dreamed of because he didn't have it for himself. By grieving my fantasy, I was able to release my impossible expectations and found an appreciation of the relationship we have, instead of the hurt and disappointment of the one we didn't, and couldn't have.

Visiting my family of origin and writing my book, *Mistaken Identity,* has changed my heart and helped me heal. I also recognize that my parents

> "Father and "son - both proud, both stubborn, more alike than either of them were prepared to admit. A lifetime spent building emotional barriers; they are difficult to break down. And now the time has come, and it's too late... it's a difficult moment. It's a lonely one."
> ~*Star Trek: The Next Generation,* TV series

gave me the perfect training ground for my spiritual evolution that I now share with the world. Letting go of the old stories through forgiveness and self-awareness has given me a new perspective.

∞

Gratitude

Over the years, I've found more and more gratitude for the small and simple things in my life: the wind on my face, the air I breathe, a walk on a hot sandy beach, the smell of the ocean, the majesty of mountains or golden prairie fields. The laughter and sadness of loving relationships, playing with Sharona, morning meditation, my comfy home, fresh food on the table, music that touches my spirit, and living in a peaceful country.

When we're grateful for small treasures, opportunities, and insights in life, we become magnets for abundance. Gratitude has a vibration that draws good to us and changes the way we experience life. Having an *attitude of gratitude* makes all the difference. Writing down the things we're grateful for, reflecting on them, and sharing them with others increases our appreciation and sense of well-being.

> "If the only prayer you ever say in your entire life is thank you, it will be enough."
> ~Meister Eckhart, theologian, philosopher

Each morning as I look outside, I thank the trees for providing the oxygen to breathe. Then I thank the sun, moon, stars, and gravity. I appreciate wildlife, birds, and insects—without all of this, life would not exist. There is no "me" outside of the rest of the universe. Next, I give gratitude for the food in my fridge, my laptop, car, TV, and other belongings. I then give thanks for my health of mind, body, and spirit. Finally, I thank Spirit for all the loving relationships in my life, ending with Sharona. I then say, "Thank you, God. Now let's go have a great day!"

∞

A Declaration of Commitment to Truth, Love, and Peace

"I am thankful for everything in my life. The air I breathe, the people I love, the people who love me, the food I eat are all gifts from the Universe."

145

AWAKENING PRACTICE 4

THE PRESENT MOMENT

꩜ ꩜
---

*Access to our Higher Power begins with
the present moment, the* Now.

꩜ ꩜

Healing is a journey of learning how to best live with our past in the present moment. Many forget that only in the Now can we courageously face our shame, fears, imperfections, and other illusions of our mistaken identity. Had I not made the present moment my primary purpose, I wouldn't have found lasting recovery.

> "See, memory is an illusion—it's all gone—so everything you know about, that makes an impression on you, is no longer there. That memory has got you hooked—it holds you to the past, and it holds you to death. But on the other hand, what is life, except there is a memory, except there is an echo. So, the course of time is much like a ship in the ocean that leaves a wake behind it, which tells us where the ship has been, the same way as the past and our memory of the past tells us what we have done. The important thing to remember in this illustration is that the wake doesn't drive the ship. So you see, if you insist on being determined by the past, that's your game. But the fact of the matter is, it all starts right now." ~*Alan Watts, author, speaker*

Knowing that I steer the boat and the past is the wake behind it helped me develop more compassion for myself. The messages from my subconscious mind telling me to beat myself up also began to lessen.

The recovery slogans, One Day at a Time and Just for Today, encourage us to stay in the present moment. The present moment is all there is. It gives us access to our Awakened Consciousness. Our biggest challenge to being in the present moment is our mind. Because the ego-mind can only exist in the future or past, it becomes uncomfortable when we practice being in the Now.

> "Yesterday is gone. Tomorrow has not yet come. We have only today. Let us begin."
> -Mother Teresa, nun, missionary

When we relinquish all inner resistance to life's natural flow, the present moment becomes our friend. Go figure.

∞

We Are Not Our Past

The past was my prison. I didn't know the event at hand wasn't the reason I flew off the handle but rather a reaction to a wound from the past that hadn't healed. Most of my relapses were past induced. I would replay my struggles, heartbreaks, loneliness, and failures over and over again to the point of insanity, and then need to escape. My addiction to replaying these bad memories wreaked havoc in my life because I attached my identity to them. As spiritual warriors, we must take an honest look at our history with fresh eyes to find awakening.

Completing step four and sharing step five from the twelve-step programs helped me recognize my mistaken identity. You'll discover and understand more about yourself by taking step four, "We made a searching and fearless moral inventory of ourselves" and step five, "We admitted to God, to ourselves, and to another human being the exact nature of our wrongs."

My unhealed past strengthened my mistaken identity and came to live in what Eckhart Tolle calls the "pain-body," an accumulation of unresolved emotional pain from the thoughts and emotions carried forward in memory. We can learn from our past, but we are not our past. Let the past go and let Love steer the boat.

∞

The Only Future Is Now

In the past, my mind lived in the future. It told me that when I had a beautiful girlfriend, a great job, a new car, a superb apartment, and a year clean, I would be happy. My drive to be accepted by the world fueled my future-seeking, and I continued to relapse. I kept looking to the future for my salvation because looking within was too painful. I was never satisfied because I couldn't accept myself in the Now. Continually trying to control the future only made me more frustrated, angry, and resentful. I had to slow down and accept the present moment and myself.

I spent much of my life saying no to my fear and addiction, not realizing I needed to say yes to my recovery and love. The present moment is how we access it.

∞

A Declaration of Commitment to Truth, Love, and Peace

"I live in the present, letting the negativity of the past slip away and the future take care of itself. I take pleasure in the blessed perfection of the ever-present, eternal living moment. I'm blessed to be alive and awake in this moment."

AWAKENING PRACTICE 5

PHYSICAL EXERCISE

꧁ ꧂

If physical exercise doesn't challenge you, it doesn't change you.

꧁ ꧂

I continued to hit the gym throughout my twenty years in and out of active addiction. I've been training for thirty-four years and have been a personal trainer. If exercise alone were a recovery milestone, I would have over three decades clean.

I focused on working out the first time I was in treatment. My counselor put an immediate stop to it. He realized my fitness obsession had become a distraction, an outside solution to recovering from addiction.

Over the years I have seen many people focus their entire recovery on working out and failing to recover. While fitness was—and still is—an integral part of my recovery, I had to find a healthy balance of mind, body, and spirit.

∞

Exercise, the Brain, and Recovery

When the body moves intensely for at least twenty minutes, the brain produces a protein called the brain-derived neurotrophic factor, dopamine, endorphins, oxytocin, and serotonin. These feel-good chemicals promote pleasure and happiness.

Brain-Derived Neurotrophic Factor (BDNF) releases into the brain in response to exercise.[29] It happens when molecules and proteins smash into each other (known as neurogenesis) to create brand-new cells (neurons) in the hippocampus, the brain's center of learning and memory.[30] Exercise is instrumental in helping us with anxiety disorders, depression, and, especially, addiction. It changes us.

Dopamine. This chemical plays a role in how we feel pleasure. All drugs of abuse, from nicotine to heroin, cause a particularly powerful surge of dopamine in the nucleus accumbens. When drugs are taken in excess, it raises the bar for pleasure and means more drugs are needed to get the same high.

A lack of dopamine causes the *Gray Zone*, not feeling good or bad, just lots of gray. The Gray Zone can last up to two years after a person stops using cocaine and even longer with methamphetamine or ecstasy. It is no surprise that these addictions have such a high relapse rate. The fastest, healthy way to get the pleasure center firing off dopamine again and shorten the Gray Zone period is high-intensity exercise.

> "Dopamine also plays a role in the brain after an individual has stopped drinking. While levels tend to drop in the initial period after abstinence from alcohol consumption, they can rebound upward in the following weeks to a similarly elevated state. It ends up creating a U-shaped curve as a person travels from an unhealthily elevated reward state due to high dopamine levels down to a depressive state due to low levels and finally back to a high state. At all three points in the process, the individual is in an unhealthy condition, which may explain the mechanism that leads to relapse."[31]
>
> *–National Society of Science: Here's What Happens*
> *to Alcoholics' Brains When They Quit Drinking*

Endorphins release in the body during moments of pain, such as when we exercise and also during stressful events. They reduce pain and stress, enhance pleasure, and support the immune system. Exercise helps us with our emotional health and supports our immune system. *The Journal of Carcinogenesis & Mutagenesis*[32] has shown endorphins can lower the likelihood of developing cancer.

Serotonin contributes to well-being and happiness. It's also responsible for regulating mood, appetite, and the sleep/wake cycle. It's often deficient in those with depression and addiction. Combining exercise with sunlight and a healthy diet can increase serotonin to healthy levels.

∞

Exercise Builds a Tough Mindset

Exercise teaches us how to be with pain, without escape or avoidance, an excellent lesson for anyone in recovery. Even a short period of movement helps us concentrate, think more clearly, and function better. Those new to recovery will especially appreciate how it helps them relax.

I call exercise *action meditation*, as it unblocks or moves negative energies as we concentrate on our breath and stay in the Now.

∞

Make Fitness a Lifestyle Change

1) Whenever I don't want to work out, I ask myself what I call the power question: "Have you ever said to yourself after your workout, 'I wish I hadn't worked out today?' " The answer is always no. I will always feel good after a workout, it's science. You will, too. Ask yourself the power question to keep exercise as a consistent, non-negotiable part of your life.

2) "Anchoring" is Anthony Robbins' strategy that acknowledges the hard work and benefits of exercise and helps reinforce fitness intentions. We anchor by recognizing the difference between how we feel at the beginning and the end of our workout, once again reinforcing how much better we feel when we exercise. Add self-praise at the end of your activity to strengthen this further. I usually do this on the way to my car.

3) Some things work better together. Exercising with another person or fitness community increases your accountability and enjoyment.

4) Seek advice from experts in the field.

5) Easy does it, but do it. Don't be in a rush to get in shape. Stick with exercise for the long run to get results.

6) Variety, as they say, is the spice of life. Alternating and trying different forms of exercise will help you keep your commitment.

∞

Exercise can boost our health and extend lifespan;[33] it lowers our risk of lung cancer, colon cancer, heart problems, obstructive pulmonary conditions, stroke, kidney disease, diabetes, and Alzheimer's and Parkinson's diseases.[34] Walking three hours a week lowers a woman's risk of stroke by 43 percent.[35] After more than thirty years of lifting weights, I still love to push myself until my tank is empty, going beyond what my mind thinks I can do. A person can build muscle and get in shape at any age.

> "You are born into this world with a set of genetics, half from mum, half from pops. Those genes expect you to run, jump, throw, tumble, dance, fight, flee, stalk, carry, build, wrestle, stroll, climb, drag, hike, and sprint. You are meant to be active. Really active."
> ~Robb Wolf, research biochemist, health expert, author

Exercise moves our negative energy, opening channels for a greater connection to the Source. It's essential to find and incorporate new ways to feel good about ourselves, especially in early recovery. Exercise does this for us.

> Learn more with my video Holistic Recovery.
> *https://youtu.be/opjQgfZWvWM.*

A Declaration of Commitment to Truth, Love, and Peace

"My good health is key to healing my addictive brain and to a joyful life. I will make exercise a regular part of my life."

AWAKENING PRACTICE 6

NUTRITIOUS FOOD

Eating healthy foods is part of relapse prevention.

When I was in active addiction and, later in early recovery, I used food like I used drugs. After days without eating, I binged on greasy foods, soft drinks, candy, and chocolate. It made me feel *temporarily* better. I had no idea that I was responding to my craving brain with another powerful substance.

Many people in recovery gain weight by substituting food for their substance of choice, increasing their likelihood of high blood pressure,

> "The brain chemistry that drives the addict to seek pleasure beyond the point of satiety is similar, whether the user favors Jack Daniels or Jack-in-the-Box."
> ~Dr. Vera Taman, medical director, food addiction specialist, author

type 2 diabetes, heart disease, and self-esteem issues. The second-largest addiction in North America is food addiction. It needs to be treated like any other addiction, not as a lack of willpower.

Many treatment centers pay little attention to the importance of healthy, nutrient-dense foods. Even AA's big book does not mention healthy eating, and we rarely discuss nutrition in meetings where it's considered an outside issue.

Tommy Rosen says, "There is an intimate connection between what you eat and how you think, feel, and behave. Your diet correlates directly with the way your life unfolds. Food is not an outside issue when it comes to any form of addiction. It is one of the core issues. Therefore, any holistic approach to recovery must include an in-depth look at your relationship with food."

Not only does food affect how we feel about ourselves, but unhealthy foods can promote relapse by triggering the pleasure chemical dopamine in the same way that drugs and alcohol do.

∞

Processed Sugar: A Dangerous Drug

Big corporations disguise sugar with multiple, often unpronounceable names—sucrose, high-fructose corn syrup, barley malt, dextrose, maltose, and rice. Soda, fruit juices, energy drinks, and most processed foods are loaded with sugar. Do you *think low-fat, natural, organic*, mean *healthy*? Think again. The second ingredient in many low-fat and low-calorie yogurts and energy/nutrition or breakfast bars is sugar.

Sugar, like drugs, alcohol, and other addictive substances and behaviors, produces a rush as it increases our brain's dopamine level to soothe our emotions. A crash follows and a desire for more of the same. Eating lots of sugar helps keep the memory of our addiction

> "Sugar is as addictive as cocaine."[36]
> ~Anna Schaefer and Kareem Basin

alive. Scan ingredient labels to make sure sugar, honey, corn syrup, and other sugars are listed fifth or later.

By the way, our bodies respond to white flour in much the same way it does to sugar. Without the bran and germ found in whole wheat, white flour becomes sugar in the gut.

∞

The Brain-Gut Connection

By the time we seek help with addiction, our bodies are malnourished, screaming for essential nutrients. The good news is that we can kick-start our healing process, reduce cravings, shorten mood swings, and lessen physical and emotional pain by eating healthy, whole foods, and nutritional supplements. Addiction affects our brains, and it's why nutrition plays a significant role in our minds and bodies' optimal health. Experts refer to this as the brain-gut connection.

Healing foods can prevent, reverse, and even cure disease. Eat smart, feel good!

∞

Feed Recovery

You'll find healthy whole foods around the perimeter of a typical grocery store and processed foods, typically loaded with unhealthy amounts of white flour, salt, sugar, chemical and "natural" flavors, colors, and preservatives in the store's center aisles.

American food writer and activist Michael Pollan says don't buy food at the same place you buy fuel for your car, and "eat food, mostly plants, not too much." By this, he means eat things previous generations would recognize as food (goodbye, frozen pizza pops!) in moderation.

> "Ninety-two percent of North Americans are deficient in one or more essential vitamins and minerals, 80 percent are deficient in vitamin D, and more than 99 percent are deficient in the essential omega-3 fatty acids."
> ~Dr. Mark Hyman, physician, founder and director
> of The UltraWellness Center, author

Make what you put on your fork support your recovery. Try a whole-foods diet for thirty days. You'll find out how much healthy foods can change your life for the better.

"Let food be thy medicine and medicine be thy food."
-Hippocrates, the father of medicine, born 460 BC

∞

A Declaration of Commitment to Truth, Love, and Peace

"I will nourish myself with life-enhancing foods that nourish every cell in my body. I will choose foods that support my recovery, increase my vibration frequency, and open me up to higher levels of consciousness."

AWAKENING PRACTICE 7

COMMITMENT

─────────────── ✌ ✍ ───────────────

How we start our day helps us stay in the day.

─────────────── ✌ ✍ ───────────────

Every morning another 86,500 seconds (1,440 minutes) is deposited into our "human life account." At the end of each day, it's withdrawn. No refunds. Time is one of our most valuable resources. Once the time is gone, it's gone for good. Unlike other resources, such as genetics, natural talents, intelligence, education, and money, we all have the same amount of time each day. It's the only aspect of our lives where we are all equal. It's the single element over which we have some control.

To achieve the life I dreamed of, I had to learn to use my time wisely. I found consistently following a daily routine the best way to support my spiritual, emotional, mental, and physical growth. Making commitments to ourselves and keeping them helps reprogram the subconscious mind and undo our mistaken identity.

> "You'll never change your life until you change something you do daily. The secret of your success is found in your daily routine."
> —John C. Maxwell, author, coach, speaker

I begin each day with meditation, prayer, and gratitude to continue building a loving, trusting relationship with the God of my understanding. I sometimes include Self-Inquiry at the end of my meditation.

Thirty minutes before I go to sleep, I review my day, consider if there are amends I need to make, and then list three good things that happened to me that day. Since we create our reality even while asleep, it's essential to avoid going to bed in a bad headspace. You'll find yourself, with practice, automatically looking for the positive experiences throughout your day.

For most of us, change is difficult. But if nothing changes, nothing changes. I had to hold myself to a higher standard or miss an awakening of consciousness and lasting recovery.

> Learn more with my video,
> How to Wire Good Memories.
> *https://youtu.be/cUyXKlGvpLw.*

∞

Support Meetings

I currently attend one meeting a week; it's my way to give back still. I have a homegroup, a sponsor, and I sponsor others.

∞

Personal Fitness Program

I work out at a gym four times a week. I may do free weights, interval training, and powerlifting in one workout or on different days. I change my workouts to keep them interesting and make sure I exercise all my muscles. Cardio burns fat optimally at the end of the workout, so I do at least twenty minutes then—a little nugget for everyone.

Exercise is a must for me. I love to run, bike, swim, and in-line skate for my cardio workout.

∞

Current Dietary Approach

In 2019, when my awakened consciousness recognized animals as conscious beings, I switched from a paleo diet to one which is mostly plant-based.

I've also been practicing intermittent fasting for the past three years. Intermittent fasting is eating all meals within eight hours, then fasting for the remaining sixteen hours.

Good nutrition and eating habits are vital to our health, recovery, and how we feel about ourselves and others. Even eating the best diet doesn't mean getting all the right minerals and vitamins. I recommend that people research to find a diet and supplements that work for them.

∞

A Declaration of Commitment to Truth, Love, and Peace

"I will have morning and evening rituals to build a better relationship with myself and the God of my understanding. I will do it until it becomes part of me."

SECTION E

CONCLUSION

THE WAY WE END STIGMA

〜◎ ◎〜

Recovery is the new cool. Join us, and experience it for yourself!

〜◎ ◎〜

Over 72,000 people died of drug overdoses in the U.S. in 2018,[37] more than all the deaths attributed to motor vehicle accidents, homicides, and suicides combined. In Canada, as of 2017, opiate overdose deaths alone were expected to reach a new high of approximately 4,000.[38] Cigarettes kill more than 480,000 people in the United States each year[39] and 37,000 in Canada.[40] Alcohol is responsible for about 88,000 deaths (approximately 62,000 men and 2,600 women die annually from alcohol-related causes) in the U.S.[41] and 6,700 in Canada annually.[42] Over 40 million North Americans[43] age twelve and up meet the clinical criteria for nicotine, alcohol, or other drug addiction. These are grim statistics with human faces behind them—people with an addiction and those who love them living in fear.

The media, government, and health care industry inundate society with stories about the destruction and death of people with addictions, but this fear-based approach hasn't worked. A new paradigm is desperately needed. While fear can be a good motivator if used intelligently, it is Love that sets us free. I call this new paradigm "Recovery: The New Cool."

∞

Recovery: The New Cool

As these statistics loom, the world is simultaneously undergoing a shift in consciousness. From youth to First Nations, LGBTQ rights, the #metoo and #timesup movements to anti-bullying campaigns, mental illness awareness, and other social movements, people are waking up, standing up, and speaking out for change.

The same is happening in the recovery world. Ten percent of the North American population, meaning 23.5 million Americans[44] and three million Canadians, are in long-term recovery. Moms, dads, sons, daughters, brothers, sisters, lawyers, doctors, bankers, firefighters, police officers, politicians, movie stars, professional athletes, and artists are standing up against shame and stigmatization.

Anonymity is the guiding principle of Alcoholics Anonymous when it began in 1935 and remains so for many. Today, I am an open advocate for recovery, and I'm not alone in "anonymous no more." As more people give recovery a face, the more others will feel safe and reach for recovery themselves. This is one way to end stigma.

Recovery: The New Cool includes many celebrities who have spoken up and put their faces on addiction and recovery.

Entertainers: Russell Brand, Kristen Johnston, Robert Downey Jr., Samuel L. Jackson, Zac Efron, John Goodman, Daniel Radcliffe, Kat Von D, Danny Trejo, Edie Falco, Kristen Davis, Ben Affleck, Bradley Cooper, Jim Carrey, Alec Baldwin, Bruce Willis, Colin Farrell, Rob Lowe, Jamie Lee Curtis, Ozzie, Jack and Kelly Osbourne, Jada Pinkett Smith, Gerard Butler, Eva Mendes, Lynda Carter, Craig Ferguson, Anthony Hopkins, David Letterman, Kate Moss, Dax Sheppard, Tom Hardy

Musicians: Eminem, Ringo Starr, Demi Lovato, Pete Townshend, Steven Tyler, Neil Young, James Taylor, Eric Clapton, Elton John, Keith Urban, Moby, Tim McGraw, Natalie Cole,

Macklemore, Stevie Nicks, Lana Del Ray, Pink, Joe Walsh, Bonnie Raitt

Professional Athletes: Joe Namath, Brett Favre, Charles Barkley, John Daly, Darryl Strawberry, Theoren Fleury, Chris Herren, C.C. Sabathia, Josh Hamilton, Thomas (Hollywood) Henderson

Recovery: The New Cool is further enhanced by people in long-term recovery. Tommy Rosen launched the Recovery 2.0 online conference in 2013. Its mission is to disseminate and teach the most cutting-edge information about recovering from addiction and thrive in a life of recovery. Rosen's book, *Recovery 2.0: Move Beyond Addiction and Upgrade Your Life,* supports research that recovery success increases when other modalities are used with the traditional twelve steps. Dr. Gabor Maté, author of the award-winning, bestselling book *In the Realm of Hungry Ghosts: Close Encounters with Addiction,* challenged and changed perceptions about addiction.

There are various of twelve-step recovery groups—Alcoholics Anonymous, Narcotics Anonymous, Cocaine Anonymous, Overeaters Anonymous, and Co-Dependents Anonymous—to name a few. The twelve-step approach works for millions. The established pillars of the twelve-step program are in use for many alternative support groups.

People from all walks of life are having honest conversations about how sobriety gave them a new life. The lie: once an addict or alcoholic, always one, will no longer be tolerated by either society or those with an addiction.

When we shift our focus from the suffering from addiction to the diversity of the millions in recovery, we will further de-stigmatize recovery and expand the opportunity to recognize, catalyze and celebrate it as a powerful force for awakening the world. The addiction that I thought was a curse is now a blessing.

> *We do recover! It's a great time to be in recovery.*

It continues to transform me and my life. I am committed to reaching as many people as possible to experience their recovery as the new cool. After all:

It's cool to wake up clean and sober.

It's cool to discover who we really are.

It's cool to learn that surrender is not a weakness but a place of great power.

It's cool to start each day with meditation and prayer.

It's cool to serve others who are still suffering as we once did.

It's cool to have real friends to share support, challenges, and growth.

It's cool to make amends.

It's cool to be vulnerable to other like-minded people.

It's cool to have a program of holistic recovery.

It's cool not to have to lie to ourselves or others.

It's cool to no longer run from our pain and suffering.

It's cool to discover that the light was in us all the time.

It's cool to learn how to love ourselves unconditionally.

It's cool to let go of self-centeredness and find inner peace.

In much the same way cancer, mental illness, child and sexual abuse, HIV/AIDS, and other diseases are losing their stigma, so is addiction. Healing happens with truth, the compassion of others, and the daily work of recovery and spiritual practices.

∞

A Declaration of Commitment to Truth, Love, and Peace

"I agree recovery is the new cool. What I focus on expands. I will focus my energy on the good and gratitude of recovery."

FINAL WORDS FROM MY HEART

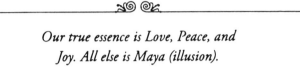

Our true essence is Love, Peace, and
Joy. All else is Maya (illusion).

Why do some people recover and others don't? The complex, multidimensional nature of addiction makes it impossible to entirely know or experience someone else's truth, especially since we receive much of our programming from infancy to seven years. As Jesuit ministers said, "Give us a child till he's seven, and we'll have him for life."

Some of us are more hardwired for addiction, but there is always a trigger. Like Dr. Gabor Maté, Eckhart Tolle, and other experts, I believe the root of addiction is invariably pain. Whether

> **"Your life doesn't reflect what you want, it reflects the program you were given."**
> ~Dr. Bruce Lipton, cell biologist, author, an international leader in epigenetics

a homeless intravenous drug user or an executive going to bed each night with half a bottle of single malt, the common denominator is the conscious and unconscious pain of your mistaken identity.

Because no two addiction cases are identical, we need to move away from the idea that clean time is the only barometer of success in recovery. Addiction is a chronic condition that affects everyone's mind, body, and spirit differently. Unfortunately, many people who can't grasp recovery will pay with their lives and it does not have to be this way.

> "Compassion is not religious business, it is human business, it is not luxury, it is essential for our own peace and mental stability, it is essential for human survival."
>
> *-Dalai Lama, spiritual teacher, politician*

After reading this book and digesting its lessons, I hope more than anything else that your takeaways will be that the surest solution to addiction is an *Awakening of Consciousness!* And the surest way to support and be part of the healing of someone else with addiction is compassion.

∞

Awakening of Consciousness

No amount of money, time, or hard work can give you a spiritual awakening. Awakening happens through Grace. We have no power over when someone is ready to accept Love as their true nature and claim their recovery. All I can say is the more we surrender and work (the Work), the more opportunities will present themselves for awakening to unfold through Grace. I had to get my silliness out of the way and allow the Life Force to unfold.

I would not be here without the compassion of my mentors, friends, and other awake beings who helped me with my struggles, mistakes, and shortcomings.

Awakening is like hide-and-seek with ourselves. Sometimes we know we are Love. Sometimes we can't find ourselves. The key is to have others remind us when we forget who we are. Without

> "We become great because others have allowed us to stand on their shoulders; no one does it alone."
>
> *~Isaac Newton, mathematician*

human connection, we are vulnerable to misery and relapse.

∞

Overcoming Darkness Transforms Us

Real transformation begins once we recognize that light exists within all darkness. Darkness then becomes our vehicle for awakening and not for destruction.

When we know this, we silence the voice of self-judgment, and our mistaken identity will begin to disappear slowly. We can then begin to walk authentically and become our best friend. As it turns out, addiction is our blessing, not the darkness we'd thought.

It's my great hope that you seek the blessings waiting for you in the darkness and lose all desire to use.

∞

Failing Spectacularly is How Greatness is Born

I woke-up and found recovery because I had failed spectacularly. I fell on my face so many times that I stopped counting. But I adjusted with each failure and learned not to make the same mistake, and when I did fail again, I readjusted and took more action.

Mistakes made me wiser, healthier, stronger, less fearful, and almost cost my life, but I never stopped believing I deserved better. I reached out to those who had what I wanted

> "You don't make mistakes. Mistakes make you."
> ~from the movie, *The Last Word*, starring Shirley MacLaine

and needed. I asked for help and even discovered that my so-called mistakes sometimes ended up being the best decision for my spiritual evolution and recovery.

Failure was never my option, even when I didn't believe it for myself because I had friends who believed it for me. Today I have the wisdom to understand there is no life without risk, failure, and living without regret.

I rose out of the ashes like a phoenix. The old me died, and I woke up to my true innate self.

There were years when nothing seemed to change, even though I was working my ass off. Then there were times when remarkable changes happened all at once.

> "It's not the critic who counts; not the man who points out how the strong man stumbles or where the doer of deeds could have done them better. The credit belongs to the person who is in the arena. Whose face is marred with dust and sweat and blood; who strives valiantly ... who at the best knows in the end the triumph of high achievement, and who at the worst, if he fails, at least fails while daring greatly ..."
>
> ~Theodore Roosevelt

By doing the work, putting one foot in front of the other, our whole system reintegrates, reconnects, heals, and reassembles within our mind, body, and spirit. When you feel challenged, remember that *before every breakthrough, there is usually a breakdown.* Don't give up! Tomorrow could be the day all your hard work comes together, and BAM, the desire to use or drink or what was your addiction is lifted, and your dream of sobriety finally becomes a reality.

∞

Our Children

Imagine a child who has rarely been smiled at, spoken to warmly and lovingly, touched gently, or played with by a parent. Imagine a child who hears constant fighting, one who grows up in an addiction environment, or a stressed single parent working two or three jobs to survive. Or another subjected to physical, sexual, and emotional abuse. These children are unlikely to develop the necessary emotional wiring to handle life, and they will form a mistaken identity, looking to external sources to make them feel better without knowing why.

Now imagine a child given a safe, nurturing environment. They are treated with kindness and respect and receive regular affirmations and actions that feed their true identity—Love.

The prevention of addiction beats the struggle of fighting addiction hands down. Growing up in a loving and safe environment can make all the difference.

$$\infty$$

Parents

Parents have never been more stressed. They need just as much help, support, and healing because raising children and living life can very difficult. Plus, they are healing things many generations deep. It will take great courage to waking up and be part of the solution.

It's never too late to recover from addiction or do your best to look after your children, giving them a better chance of not being susceptible to addiction.

Writing this book has changed my heart and helped me clear the path, so I could clearly witness my parents as the beautiful God essence they are. I have a relationship with my whole family today; it's not perfect, but it's real, and I love them all. I am truly a blessed man!

$$\infty$$

You Are Love

Serendipity so often happens on the spiritual path. As we continue to awaken spiritually, we find that the information, experience, person, thing, or opportunity we need appears at just the right time. And so it was with this book. A friend in recovery sent me the following poem by Cleo Wade, which her brother, also in recovery, had sent her. I hope it inspires you to let go of your mistaken identity and open yourself to the flawless truth: You are Love.

love never lies
shame never tells the truth
it tells you
you are not
good enough
the truth is
you are
it tells you
you have to be perfect
the truth is
you don't
it tells you
your mistakes
are fatal wounds
the truth is
you heal
it tells you
everything has fallen apart
the truth is
you will rebuild
it tells you
that you will stay sunken in despair
the truth is
you will rise
it tells you
you failed
you lost
and you got hurt

the truth is
you learned (what to do next time)
you gained (knowledge from your knockdown)
and found out (just how strong you are)
it says
you will never make it
the truth is
keep going
for
shame said
you would never
survive
and the truth is
you
are
still
here

And finally, the most common statement I hear, time and time again from my clients and one that I wrestled with myself for over 40 years:

"I have nothing to offer the world."

Yes, you do!

Every human being can serve humanity right now by being their authentic selves! Because when we are *ourselves*, we allow others to let go of their self-judgment and be *themselves*.

Nobody needs some grandiose purpose. Just Be Yourself—which means accepting Love as our true nature. It's more than enough!

> "The most precious and honorable gift you can give anyone is your authentic self."

A FINAL DECLARATION AND COMMITMENT TO TRUTH, LOVE, AND PEACE

"All is well with my soul, and so it IS!"

One Love,

Paul Noiles and my Sharona

For more information or to schedule an appointment, please visit paulnoiles.com.

AFFIRMATIVE PRAYERS

Affirmative Prayer 1

"I am radiant in body, mind, heart, and spirit. I am deeply grateful for the good in my life. I know that love guides all my relationships. I no longer choose to believe in old limitations and lack. I now see myself as the universe sees me—perfect, whole, and complete. I am worthy of the very best in life.

"I will honor my feelings, know they are not permanent, they are not who I am. They are like clouds in the sky that come and go. I am deeply relaxed because I am Peace. I am growing more positive each day. My resources come from an unlimited source. Abundance is in my life. I know all things are unfolding as they should. There are no mistakes in the spirit realm. All is well."

Affirmative Prayer 2

"I let go of all that no longer serves me. As I let go, I am healed and made whole. My life is blessed, and I am grateful for all that I have."

Affirmative Prayer 3

"I am a divine expression of a loving God, divine being, universal energy. I lay my heart at the feet of your omnipresence. I surrender to you, Almighty Loving Spirit.

"All my thoughts, words, and actions are divinely guided. A river of compassion washes away all my fears and replaces them with love. Compassion is the bridge of love, and I shall give it freely and often. The air that I breathe is your holy presence. I am growing and evolving in the ever-expanding Now.

"The universe provides for all my needs. My resources come from an unlimited Source. I am brimming with energy and overflowing with joy. I am courageous and walk with bravery, knowing there are no mistakes, only lessons for my soul's evolution. My body is healthy. My mind is brilliant. My soul is forever evolving and eternal. I am deathless. All is grace."

Affirmative Prayer 4

"I am a divine expression of a loving God, divine being, universal energy. I let go of fear. I let go of pain. I forgive and ask for forgiveness from all those I may have wronged.

"The air that I breathe is your holy presence inside of me. These creative words that I speak are my daily bread. All my thoughts, words, and actions are divinely guided. I thank you for my body that houses my eternal soul. I will honor and take care of it.

"The universe naturally and freely provides for all my needs. My mind and body are in complete alignment with the universe. I am always in the flow. I am responsible for my spiritual growth. Everything that happens is for my highest good. Love is working through me, now and always.

"With the sword of devotion, I sever the heartstrings that tie me to delusions of the mind. With the most profound love, I lay my heart at the feet of your omnipresence. I surrender to God, the Nameless Wonder, that is always with me. I do only Love's bidding."

Affirmative Prayer 5 (for those facing surgery)

"I release any anxiety or worry because all is God, all is well. My body is in perfect health and ready for the operation. My mind is clear. It knows that Love is all there is. I am at peace with life and myself. I have great faith in my surgeon and the team. I know that every cell in my body knows what to do for optimal healing.

"I am ready to have my body repaired to its perfection. I am open and receptive to all the energies in the universe. Perfect health is my divine right. I claim it now."

> You can find more affirmations at I AM Affirmation.
> https://youtu.be/Ci2FDcVZ1wY.

THE MYTHS OF ROCK BOTTOM AND WILLINGNESS

Rich Jones

In terms of "rock bottom" and willingness, I agree with all the ideas discussed to this point. Rock bottom and willingness are myths, and more people than ever are challenging these ideas. I guess that is what happens when 73,000 people die of overdoses every year. We start questioning concepts that have never before been challenged. … no research supports the legitimacy of hitting bottom as a helpful construct, at least in terms of outcomes. I'm not sure there is a more important outcome than staying alive, and we know that rock bottom directly contributes to an increase in deaths, especially in this age of fentanyl and carfentanyl. Besides, the necessity of willingness as a prerequisite for successful treatment has been entirely deconstructed by motivational interviewing.

Interestingly, despite the widespread adoption of motivational interviewing in the addiction field, providers do not practice motivational principles. For example, kicking someone out of a therapy group for using or out of a residential program for "non-compliance" is 100 percent antithetical to motivational principles. Cookie-cutter aftercare plans demanding twelve-step attendance and involvement in intensive outpatient programs do not reflect individualized client-centered programming. In addition, encouraging the family to get out of the way and wait for the bottom remains the default setting for most family advice given by professionals in this field. It begs the question: Why is this still the prevailing attitude? Furthermore, what other options are available for the family in need?

Why do the concepts of willingness and hitting bottom still carry so much weight in the addiction treatment and recovery space? The short answer is old habits die hard. The inability of groups to adopt new thinking is not unique to the addiction treatment and recovery industry. It is a human tendency to double down on the status quo when the founding paradigm is challenged. This doubling down is magnified where addiction is concerned because the stigma has walled off those with substance use disorder from the rest of society. The industry, and recovery groups, as a whole, are closed and insular. It's an echo chamber. Nothing changes because we all parrot the same talking points. The concept of hitting bottom has never been established as a legitimate therapeutic approach, yet counselors, therapists, and programs offer that advice 1,000 times a day. Right now, some parent somewhere is being told by a professional that the kid must hit bottom. Again, please understand that hitting bottom is a *slogan* thrown around at 12-step meetings. There is nothing wrong with 12-step members developing a slogan. However, this slogan tragically guides our nation's healthcare response to addiction. Hitting bottom is part of the company line, and most are not going to step outside the company line. More accurately, most are not going to go against the norms of the tribe

Stigma is another reason for the survival of hitting bottom as a guiding principle in the industry. Industry protocols have never been studied or challenged because John Q. Public couldn't care less about those with substance use disorders. "Those junkies are lucky they get any help." Therefore, ineffective and dangerous practices proceed unencumbered by oversight or evaluation. Fortunately, this is changing. Unfortunately, it took the destruction of an entire generation to prompt this change. Ironically, the nation had to hit bottom for the industry to be held accountable.

The final explanation is more complex and problematic. It does not involve individual people or individual programs, rather the system as a whole and standard operating procedures within that system. The idea of willingness fits in well with a fractured and largely ineffective treatment system. Unsuccessful experiences in treatment can be put back on the patient. For example, if someone goes to rehab and relapses shortly after discharge, it can be attributed to a lack of willingness. This self-reinforcing concept is too convenient and addictive for the industry to shake off. It works too well. It has been used for fifty years as a justification for poor outcomes. The person didn't get better not because he didn't want to get better, but because we need to develop new and creative ways of treating people.

Again, fortunately, this is all in the process of changing. The addiction treatment and recovery industry left standing ten years from now will not resemble what we have today. The transition has already started.

As they say, when the pain gets great enough, the change will be embraced. I believe we are in the middle of a great transition because the pain has gotten great enough.

I thank Paul Noiles for the opportunity to contribute to this important work. I believe Paul reflects this new way of thinking. I am proud to call him a friend.

Rich Jones

SUGGESTED RESOURCES

Addiction and Recovery

Alcoholics Anonymous, Fourth Edition, Anonymous

The Book of Secrets: 112 Meditations to Discover the Mystery Within, Osho

Chasing the Scream: The First and the Last Days of the War on Drugs, Johann Hari

Clean: Overcoming Addiction and Ending America's Greatest Tragedy, David Sheff

Codependent No More: How to Stop Controlling Others and Start Caring for Yourself, Melody Beattie

Dealing with Addiction: Why the 20th Century Was Wrong, Peter Ferentzy

Healing the Shame that Binds You, John Bradshaw

In the Realm of Hungry Ghosts, Gabor M. Maté

The Globalization of Addiction: A Study in Poverty of the Spirit, Bruce K. Alexander

Narcotics Anonymous Basic Text, Fellowship of Narcotics Anonymous

Recovery 2.0: Move Beyond Addiction and Upgrade Your Life, Tommy Rosen

The Unbroken Brain, Maia Szalavitz

Spiritual Awakening

Bhagavad Gita (A New Translation), Stephen Mitchell

A Course in Miracles, scribed by Helen Schucman

The Dark Side of the Light Chasers, Debbie Ford

Enlightenment is Your Nature: The Fundamental Difference Between Psychology, Therapy, and Meditation, Osho

Man's Search for Meaning, Viktor E. Frankl

A New Earth: Awakening to Your Life's Purpose, Eckhart Tolle

The Power of Now: A Guide to Spiritual Enlightenment, Eckhart Tolle

A Return to Love, Marianne Williamson

The Untethered Soul, Michael Singer

Vaster Than Sky, Greater Than Space, Mooji

The Way of Liberation: A Practical Guide to Spiritual Enlightenment, Adyashanti

The Wisdom of Insecurity: A Message for an Age of Anxiety, Alan Watts

Mindfulness and Meditation, Eco-Institute's: *ecoinstitute.org/ meditation/141-benefits of meditation*

Experts for Inspiration

Richard L. Jones, counselor, therapist, and coach recoverycartel. com/about/

Tommy Rosen, yoga teacher, Recovery 2.0 founder r20.com

Dr. Gabor Maté, physician, addiction and trauma expert, author drgabormate.com

Eckhart Tolle, spiritual teacher, author eckharttolle.com

ENDNOTES

1   Gabor Maté. *In the Realm of Hungry Ghost.* (Toronto: Random House, 2012), pg. 129-130.
2   Maia Szalavitz. (Modified June 14, 2017). "Never Before Has Our Approach To Drugs Improved So Much, So Fast." *Pacific Standard.* psmag.com/social-justice/never-before-has-ou r-approach-to-drugs-improved-so-much-so-fast (last accessed 20 November 2020).
3   Bruce K. Alexander. *The Globalization of Addiction: A Study in Poverty of the Spirit.* (Oxford: Oxford University Press. 2010), pg. 62-63.
4   Chopra, Deepak. *Overcoming addictions* (New York: Three Rivers Press, 1997), pg. 4
5   Lawrence Robinson, Melinda Smith, Jeanne Segal. (n.d.) "Dual Diagnosis: Substance Abuse and Mental Health." *HelpGuide.* helpguide.org/articles/addictions/substance-abuse-and-mental-health.htm/ (last accessed 1 October 2020).
6   Howard J. Shaffer. (July 2011). "How Addiction Hijacks the Brain." *Harvard Health Publishing.* health.harvard.edu/newsletr_article/how-addiction-hijacks-the-brain (last accessed 20 November 2020).
7   Citing data from Rima Shore *Rethinking the Brain: New Insights into Early Development.* (New York, NY: Families and Work Institute, Rev. 2001)
8   Janice Wood. (August 8, 2018). "What's Your Earliest Memory?" *Psych Central.* psychcentral.com/news/2014/01/26/

whats-your-earliest-memory/64982.html (last accessed 2 November 2020).

9   Jane Liebschutz, et. al. (April 22, 2002). "The Relationship Between Sexual and Physical Abuse and Substance Abuse Consequences." *National Institute of Health Journal of Substance Abuse Treatment, (3); 121-128.* ncbi.nlm.nih.gov/pmc/articles/PMC4861063/ (last accessed 10 November 2020).

10 John Bradshaw. *Healing the Shame that Binds You.* (Deerfield Beach, FL: Health Communications, Inc., 1988), pg. 29

11 Peter Ferentzy. *Dealing with Addiction: Why the 20ᵗʰ Century Was Wrong.* (Toronto, Canada: Self-Published, May 23, 2011), pg. 1-2

12 Michael A. Singer. *The Untethered Soul: The Journey Beyond Yourself.* (Oakland, CA: New Harbinger Publications, 2007), pg. 8

13 Bill Wilson's Experience with LSD https://aaagnostica. org/2015/05/10/bill-wilsons-experience-with-lsd/ (last accessed 20 November 2020).

14 Byron Katie. *A Friendly Universe: Sayings to Inspire and Challenge You.* (New York, NY: TarcherPerigee, 2013), pg. 5

15 R.I. Damian, M. Spengler, A. Sutu, & B.W. Roberts, B.W. (2019). "Sixteen Going on Sixty-Six: A Longitudinal Study of Personality Stability and Change Across 50 Years." *Journal of Personality and Social Psychology, 117*(3), 674–695. https://psycnet.apa.org/record/2018-39707-001

16 Anne Helmenstine. (December 2019) "Chemical Composition of the Human Body." *ThoughtCo.* https://www.thoughtco. com/chemical-composition-of-the-human-body-603995 (last accessed 12 November 2020).

17 Clara Moskowitz. (November 1, 2007). "Fact or Fiction?: Energy Can Neither Be Created Nor Destroyed." *Scientific American.* scientificamerican.com/article/energy-can-neithe r-be-created-nor-destroyed/ (last accessed 20 November 2020)

18 https://www.brucekalexander.com/articles-speeches/rat-park (last accessed 20 November 2020)

19 Corrine Rees. (November 1, 2007). Childhood Attachment. *British Journal of General Practice 57 (544): 920-922.* ncbi. nlm.nih.gov/pmc/articles/PMC2169321/ (last accessed 20 November 2020).

20 Beattie, Melody. *Codependent No More: How to Stop Controlling Others and Start Caring for Yourself.* (Center City, MN: Hazelden, 1986), pg. 63

21 Marianne Williamson. *A Return to Love: Reflections on the Principles of 'A Course in Miracles.'* (New York, NY: HarperCollins, 1992) pg.165

22 *Osho.* (, 2012). *The Book of Secrets:112 Meditations to Discover the Mystery.* (New York, NY: St. Martin's Griffin, Rev. 2012)

23 Substance Abuse and Mental Health Services Administration (US). (2016). "Early Intervention, Treatment, and Management of Substance Use Disorders." NCBI, Chap. 4. ncbi.nlm.nih. gov/books/NBK424859/

24 Lopez, German. (March 15, 2018). "Anonymous Works for Some People. A New Study Suggests the Alternatives Do Too." *Vox.* vox.com/science-and-health/2018/3/5/17071690/ alcoholics-anonymous-aa-smart-lifering-study (last accessed 20 November 2020).

25 Britta K. Hölze, et. al. (November 10, 2010). "Mindfulness Practice Leads to Increases in Regional Brain Gray Matter Density." ncbi.nlm.nih.gov/pmc/articles/PMC3004979/ (last accessed 20 November 2020).

26 Eco-Institute. (n.d.) "How Meditation Conquers Addiction." eocinstitute.org/meditation/7-reasons-meditatio n-can-naturally-beat-addiction/ (last accessed 20 November 2020).

27 Adyashanti. *The Way of Liberation.* (San Jose, CA: Open Gate Sangha. 2013. Pg. 30

28 Adi Jaffe (October 16, 2011). "Mindfulness, Meditation, and Addiction." *Psychology Today.* psychologytoday.com/ca/blog/all-about-addiction/201110/mindfulness-meditation-and-addiction (last accessed 20 November 2020).

29 Sama F. Sleiman, et. al. (June 2, 2016). "Exercise Promotes the Expression of Brain-Derived Neurotrophic Factor (BDNF) Through the Action of the Ketone Body B-Hydroxybutyrate." ncbi.nlm.nih.gov/pmc/articles/PMC4915811/ (last accessed 20 November 2020).

30 "11 Ways To Grow New Brain Cells and Stimulate Neurogenesis." (2014). *Mental Health Daily.* mentalhealthdaily.com/201 3/03/05/11-ways-to-grow-new-brain-cells-and-stimulate-neurogenesis/ (last accessed 20 November 2020).

31 IFLScience. (March 3, 2016). "Here's What Happens to Alcoholics' Brains When They Quit Drinking." *IFLScience.* iflscience.com/brain/what-happens-alcoholics-brain s-when-they-quit-drinking/ (last accessed 20 November 2020).

32 T.G. Shrihari. (July 24, 2017). "Endorphins on Cancer: A Novel Therapeutic Approach." *Journal of Carcinogenesis & Mutagenesis, 8:4.* https://www.omicsonline.org/open-access/endorphins-on-cancer--a-novel-therapeutic-approach-2157-2518-1000298.php?aid=91929 (last accessed 20 November 2020).

33 Anna Azvolinsky. (May 30, 2013). Exercise "Boosts Life Expectancy, Study Finds." *LiveScience.* livescience.com/3672 3-exercise-life-expectancy-overweight-obese.html (last accessed 20 November 2020).

34 Harvard Health Publishing. (July 2016). "Does Regular Exercise Reduce Cancer Risk?" *Harvard Health Publishing.* health.harvard.edu/exercise-and-fitness/does-regular-exercis e-reduce-cancer-risk (last accessed 20 November 2020).

35 Michelle Castillo. (January 4, 2013), "Walking Three Hours per Week May Lower Women's Stroke Risk. *Columbia*

Broadcasting System News. cbsnews.com/news/walking-3-hour s-per-week-may-lower-womens-stroke-risk/ (last accessed 20 November 2020).

36   Anna Schaefer and Kareem Yasin (April 30 2020). "Experts Agree: Sugar Might Be as Addictive as Cocaine." https://www.healthline.com/health/food-nutrition/experts-is-sugar-addictive-drug (last accessed 20 November 2020).

37   Erin Durkin. (August 16, 2018). "U.S. Drug Overdose Deaths Rose to Record 72,000 Last Year, Data Reveals." *The Guardian.* (last accessed DATE. MONTH, YEAR). https://www.theguardian.com/us-news/2018/aug/16/us-drug-overdose-deaths-opioids-fentanyl-cdc (last accessed 20 November 2020).

38   The Canadian Press. (December 19, 2017). "Opioid Deaths in Canada Expected to Hit 4,000 By by End Of of 2017." *Canadian Broadcast Corporation.* CBC News. http://www.cbc.ca/news/health/opioid-deaths-canada-4000-projected-2017-1.4455518 (last accessed 20 November 2020).

39   Fast Facts | Fact Sheets | CDCCenters for Disease Control and Prevention. (n.d.) "Fast Facts: Smoking and Tobacco Use." https://www.cdc.gov/tobacco/data_statistics/fact_sheets/fast_facts/index.htm (last accessed 20 November 2020).

40   Media Opportunity: the Canadian Cardiovascular CongressGovernment of Canada. "The Scoop." (January 10, 2008). *Canada.ca.* https://www.canada.ca/en/health-canada/services/health-concerns/tobacco/youth-zone/scoop.html (last accessed 20 November 2020).

41   The National Center on Addiction and Substance Abuse at Columbia University. (2012). "Addiction Medicine: Closing the Gap Between Science and Practice." thenationalcouncil.org/wp-content/uploads/sites/7/2016/02/Addiction-medicine-closing-the-gap-between-science-and-practice.pdf?daf=375ateTbd56 (last accessed 20 November 2020).

42   Diane Reily (November 1998). "Drugs and Drug Policy in Canada: A Brief Review and Commentary." *Canadian*

Foundation for Drug Policy & International Harm Reduction.
https://sencanada.ca/content/sen/committee/362/ille/rep/
rep-nov98-e.htm (last accessed 20 November 2020).

43   The American Society of Addiction Medicine. (Addiction
Medicine 2012). "ASAM Releases New Definition of Addiction."
ASAM Newsletter 26:3. https://www.centeronaddiction.org/
sites/default/files/files/2012-annual-report.pdf. (last accessed
20 November 2020).

44   The Partnership at Drugfree.org & the New York Office of
Alcoholism and Substance Abuse Services. (March 6, 2012).
"Survey: Ten Percent of American Adults Report Being in
Recovery from Substance Abuse or Addiction." https://drugfree.
org/newsroom/news-item/survey-ten-percent-of-america
n-adults-report-being-in-recovery-from-substance-abuse-or-
addiction/(last accessed 20 November 2020).